When one person dreams alone,
it is only a dream...
When we dream together
it is the beginning of reality.

AMERICAN CENTURY TOWERS IN THE MIST

Looking out my window one morning
just before dawn,
I saw our American Century Towers
rising out of the clouds and mist as if in a dream.
As I took this picture, I thought of all of the dreams
that we're building together
as an American Century family.

*If you don't think tomorrow is going
to be better than today, why get up?
You've got to believe each new day is
going to be better, and you have to
be determined to make it so.
If you are determined, then certainly...
the best is yet to be.*

The Best is Yet to Be
First Edition
© 2007 by Stowers Innovations, Inc.
All rights reserved. Printed in the United States of America.

No part of this book may be used or reproduced in any manner whatsoever
except in the case of reprints in the context of reviews.
For information write:
Stowers Innovations, Inc.
4500 Main Street, Kansas City, Missouri 64111-7709

ISBN 978-0-9629788-7-6
Library of Congress Card Number: 2006906691

The Best is Yet to Be®

BY
JAMES E. STOWERS
WITH
JACK JONATHAN

Discover the good life!™

STOWERS INNOVATIONS
— INC —

An American Century Company

NULLA ROSA SINE SPINA:
There is No Rose Without Thorns

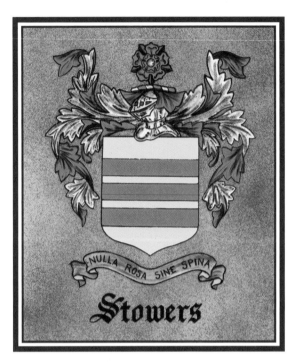

*T*he motto of the Stowers family exemplifies Jim's special achievement: the fruit of one's effort grows out of a bush with thorns. Many people are not aware of the many challenges that stood in the way of Jim's success. Every time he encountered an obstacle, Jim was determined that he could overcome it with the strong belief that his best times were still ahead of him.

Jim's favorite metaphor is that an acorn, planted and cared for, slowly matures into a beautiful tree. Just as it takes a long time for an oak tree to grow from an acorn, so it takes a long time and a lot of determination for someone to become financially independent.

There is yet a third image which illustrates Jim's achievement: scientists have recently discovered that a big tree with deep roots will extend its roots up to provide sustenance for smaller trees whose roots have yet to grow down far enough to get water. Likewise, the financial resources Jim and Virginia created over 50 years are like the big tree, supporting the Stowers Institute for Medical Research beyond their lifetimes.

Jack Jonathan

Introduction

By John C. Danforth

The story of Jim Stowers, Jr. is an inspirational lesson for all of us that we can accomplish great things if our focus is not on ourselves but on helping others.

A person of genuine modesty, Jim has never been a self-promoter. His ambition has been to be a force for good in his community and in the world, not to win credit for himself. His business philosophy has been that if he helped others become financially successful, he would become successful. Because of the combination of his success and his personal humility, he is one of Kansas City's best kept secrets.

His business philosophy has borne fruit. American Century employs more than 2,000 people and manages the assets of over two million investors. Without doubt, that is a success story. But Jim has not been content to rest on the laurels of his accomplishments in business. Where many people would be satisfied with reflecting on past achievements, Jim Stowers has set his sights on future goals.

The title of this book is telling, for Jim Stowers is relentlessly optimistic. He is convinced that the best is yet to be. In his words, "If you don't think that tomorrow is going to be better than today, why get up?" By "better" he does not mean a better life for himself. He means a better world for all of us.

Since 1999, when Jim and Virginia Stowers broke ground for the Stowers Institute for Medical Research, their dream has been to create in Kansas City one of the best biomedical research institutes in the world, not only to bring distinction to their home town but to help find the cure to terrible diseases that afflict countless millions of people. Nearly all of us have experienced the sense of hopelessness when we or those we love are diagnosed as having what are thought to be incurable diseases such as diabetes, Parkinson's, Alzheimer's, cancer or the illness that claimed the life of my brother Don, ALS or Lou Gehrig's disease. To us, Jim Stowers has offered a "Hope for Life."

In only five years, the Stowers Institute for Medical Research has put together an internationally renowned team of scientists led by Dr. Bill Neaves and Dr. Robb Krumlauf, that works in a magnificent scientific environment and in an atmosphere of collegiality, to advance Jim's "Hope for Life" vision. Thanks to Jim, Kansas City is a recognized center of biomedical research.

By his unassuming generosity, Jim Stowers is, indeed, offering hope to countless people that excellent research will relieve the suffering of life-taking diseases. Beyond the hope of healthier and longer lives, he offers all of us an example of selfless generosity, of using ones' God-given talents in the service of a better world.

John C. Danforth

Acknowledgements

Creating this book with Jim Stowers reminds me of attending the preview of a play and meeting the two principal actors. Their success was facilitated by many people, including the supporting cast, technical staff, stage-hands, front office workers, publicity staff and many others.

In creating *The Best Is Yet To Be*, there were many stages of development starting with essays from the early 1980's, followed by additional observations that were written in response to unfolding events. Along the way, we have relied on many people who critically read those early attempts, as well as at least eight versions of our "finished" typescripts.

We greatly appreciate the time and care of our reviewers and editors: Dick Brown, Judy Jost, Irving Kuraner, Whitey Kuhn, Miriam McCartney, Bill Neaves, Nancy O'Neill, Dave Tucker and Dave Welte. Jonathan Thomas read the last two versions with great care and provided us with several insightful comments which greatly improved the book.

Among those who contributed to creating this book, we are deeply grateful to the extraordinary effort of Dr. Sheelagh Manheim, whose enthusiasm and initiative helped us revisit our early starts with fresh insights.

The production of *The Best Is Yet To Be* was made possible thanks to the Stowers Innovations' team effort of Sam Goller, Alexis Preston, Kuhn and Wittenborn Advertising, Morningstar Communications Company and Addington Design.

We invited longtime members of the American Century network to share with us their experiences dating back to the early beginnings. We are grateful to Carrie Hill who assembled the early documents, coordinated the transcription of our interviews with Abbie Anderson and organized our lively "Kitchen Cabinet" session with: Betty Crooker, Mary Jo Browne, Lois Cole, Martha Miller, Debbie McMullin, Kathy Jantsch, Alice Boinski and Terry Featherston.

Archival company photographs and material were essential to the success of our book. We would like to thank Caleb Fey, Marie Jennings and Melissa Precht, who searched and gathered the archival material that helped to illustrate the events in Jim's life.

Several people who have been close to Jim and have worked with him for many years were gracious enough to agree to be interviewed: Irving Kuraner, Dennis von Waaden, Jack Urie, Bill Neaves and Dick Brown. Dick Stowers not only spent time with us being interviewed, but sent us some family documents that have enhanced our coverage of Jim's early history.

Virginia, Jim's champion and partner, read and reread the many versions of the typescript and provided us with insightful comments. She also graciously agreed to be interviewed.

Table of Contents

XII

Formative Years

Deep Roots

BY JACK JONATHAN

Few people realize how deeply connected the name Stowers is with the early pioneers who left an indelible mark on the Kansas City landscape. The amazing story of initiative, passion, determination and courage that are the roots of this city is evident in the contributions of the Evans, McGee and Stowers families.

The pioneering spirit that inspires the Stowers today finds its origin in the genes that coursed through the veins of the Evans and the McGees who came to this area nearly 200 years ago.

One striking feature of the Evans-Stowers families is their passion to educate not only their young men, but also their young women. When Jim Stowers married Virginia Glascock, he followed in the footsteps of his ancestors, marrying a woman who would be his true partner and who shared his values and passion for helping others. She has been described as "a unique blend of pioneer woman and modern lady."

Colonel McGee

John Evans, who came with his parents to Clay County, Missouri, from Illinois in 1818, is one of the first pioneers connected to Jim's family. He built the first hotel in Kansas City and established the first ferry to cross the river from Kansas City to Clay County. Nearly 140 years later, James Evans Stowers, Jr. demonstrated his pioneering spirit when, against the advice of the banking community, he created a mutual fund company which now ranks among the largest in the nation.

Who would have thought that this young man, whose education was in medicine rather than business, would create for so many the opportunity to become financially independent? His well-respected company, American Century, started with five men in the basement of a bank. Today it manages assets of over $100 billion, employs more than 2,000 people and has over two million investors.

17

Jim Stowers, the innovator, is also a true "son" of his great grandfather, James Calvin Evans, who was a nationally respected horticulturalist. Among Evans' accomplishments were the establishment of a fruit company, originating four new varieties of fruits and a 30 year tenure as president of the Missouri Horticultural Society.

Another of Jim's ancestors, Colonel McGee, had such a passion for the future of Kansas City that he was often seen with a brass band on the city's levee attempting to persuade incoming passengers to stay instead of continuing on west. Like the Colonel, Jim is one of the city's greatest advocates, choosing to keep his company on Main Street in Kansas City, instead of moving to Wall Street.

Jim and Virginia, who are both cancer survivors, had a great dream to create a medical research institute that would give hope for a better life to all mankind. This dream became a reality with the creation of the Stowers Institute for Medical Research. Once again, Jim went against the warnings of "experts" who could not envision Kansas City as home base for a premier

The rock ledge of the riverfront between Delaware and Grand Avenue, which was the first wharf of the "Town of Kansas." From a drawing made in 1852.

THE RIVER BORN TOWN

Clay County Court House at Liberty, Missouri.

medical research institution. The Institute, which opened its doors in 2000, already has achieved an international reputation, confirming Jim's belief that the Greater Kansas City area might one day be known as BioMed Valley.

Even now, in his 80's, Jim continues to lead the way with his innovations. Most recently, Jim has created an original concept for managing the Stowers Institute's endowment to protect its future financial assets. Throughout his career, Jim's leadership has been anchored by his deep roots and values. However, he also firmly believes in surrounding himself with the very best people, who work well as a team, share his vision and support his innovative approaches to making his dreams a reality.

Chapter 1

Family Influence

A tender moment with Dad.

Chapter 1

TO THE GLORY OF MY FATHER

Mary and Sterling Stowers had only one child, my father, James Evans Stowers. I can only imagine the care with which my well-educated grandmother nurtured my father in his early years. Later, he received a rigorous, classical secondary education at the Appleton City Military School. Like his father, my Dad studied medicine – first at the University of Missouri and then at Johns Hopkins Medical School, graduating in 1913.

The world was soon swept up in the "war to end all wars," and it is not surprising that my father signed up to fight, following in the tradition of his grandfather who fought in the Civil War. Because the United States was not yet at war, my Dad volunteered his services as a doctor with the American Red Cross in England. When the Red Cross doctors were recalled to the United States, Father went to France and served with the French Army Medical Corps on the battlefront.

His bravery was evident when, although he was injured, he continued to operate on a wounded soldier. During his service in France, he established a regional hospital where he performed over 30,000 operations. The French government decorated him with three military honors: two Croix de Guerre and the Legion of Honor Medal – a privilege accorded to few Americans.

Chapter 1

Father with his parents, Dr. Sterling Price Stowers
and Mary Evans Stowers.

For his extraordinary service to the French during World War I, Dr. Stowers received three honors: two Croix de Guerre, one with bronze stars, on April 14, 1919; and the Knight of the National Order of the Legion of Honor on September 27, 1919.

Commendation
Croix de Guerre

An excerpt, translated from the 10th Army Health Services Directorate, Order #212.

Major James E. Stowers, Medical Aide 1st Class, a volunteer in the French army, has given for the last three years, his services to innumerable wounded. An excellent surgeon, he has not ceased during this long period, his remarkable devotion and steadfastness, even under very difficult circumstances, including continuous bombardment of the hospitals in which he worked.

This officer will have the right to wear the Croix de Guerre with bronze stars.

National Order of the Legion of Honor

An excerpt, translated from the original order registered number 23.460.

The Grand Chancellor of the National Order of the Legion of Honor certifies that by decree of September 27, 1919, the President of the French Republic has awarded to Major James. E. Stowers, Medical Aide, Military Hospital at Mayence, 1st American Army, the decoration of Knight of the National Order of the Legion of Honor.

Hôpital Auxiliaire No. 43 Bis, where my father practiced surgery during World War 1.

Chapter 1

*B*orn at 2304 E. 12th Street, Kansas City, Missouri, and graduated with A.B, 1910, A.M, 1911, from the University of Missouri, Dr. Stowers took his M.D. from Johns Hopkins in 1913. He interned at St. Agnes Hospital in Baltimore and received his postgraduate training in 1914-1915 at Royal Victoria Hospital in Internal Medicine. He sailed to England on February 20, 1915 to serve under Sir William Osler at Paighnton, England in a Red Cross Hospital. After several months in a hospital where the nurses fought in the operating room, he transferred to the French Army and remained with them until November 1919. Hospitals in which he served were at Marseilles, Avignon, Chalus sur Maunes and Compeigne Hospital, under Alexis Carrel. He finally became Chief of Surgery there, with 500 beds and eight assistants.

The famous Lafayette Escadrille was one of his military assignments. He suffered a scalp wound while operating, but continued even though ordered to the rear. The French government awarded him the Legion of Honor and the Croix de Guerre. Subsequently, he received his Boards in Surgery and became a Fellow of the American College of Surgeons. He also was a member of the Western Surgical Association.

From: *Those Indomitable Surgeons of Hospital Hill,*
by Ray Snider and Bob Mathews

Chapter 1

THE INFLUENCE OF MY FATHER

In 1919, when my decorated father returned from France, he set up a medical practice in Kansas City, Missouri. Although my father had experienced the trauma of war in Europe, he was also attuned to the finer things of life. He found a good match in the educated, sophisticated Laura Smith. They were married on September 17, 1921, in Kansas City.

By then my father had developed a remarkable reputation as a surgeon and was highly respected in our community. In those days doctors usually performed surgery in several local hospitals. My father also made routine house calls because people only went to the hospital as a last resort. Today it is the other way around – doctors rarely make house calls, and people routinely go to a hospital.

I loved my dad and was extremely proud of him. Many times I went with him while he made house calls. Sometimes he even took me along to the hospital. I remember visiting with the telephone operator while my father was seeing patients.

Dad getting into his car to do his rounds, circa 1925.

Because of his profession, my father had very little time for himself or his family. Nevertheless, he was a caring father and very much aware of how he wanted my brother, Dick, and me to be raised. He and Mother felt it was important for us to get a good education. When I was old enough to do odd jobs to earn spending money, my father

Chapter 1

did not want me to work. Instead, he encouraged me to concentrate on my academic and musical studies. He also urged me to play and enjoy life while I still could.

The main focus of Dad's life was medicine ... he was not mechanically inclined. In fact, he was not adept at any of the practical things many boys associate with their fathers. One year Santa brought me an electric train. On Christmas morning, no matter how we struggled to get it started, we could not make that train run. I was told that Santa didn't remember how to put it together correctly. I had to wait until my Uncle King came for dinner. He made the train work and saved the day for Santa ... and my father.

MY MOTHER'S FAMILY HISTORY

My mother grew up in a family of innovative, enterprising people, the Smith family from New Jersey and the King family from Kentucky. Both families had made the trek west to seek new opportunities.

Mother's maternal grandparents, John and Laura Ellis King, came to Stanley, Kansas, from Kentucky in 1885. In Ottawa, Kansas, Kora Mercer King, their oldest daughter, met Richard West Smith, a graduate of the university there. Although they were married in Kentucky in 1890, Richard and Kora lived in Ottawa, Kansas, during the first years of their marriage.

By the time they moved to Kansas City in 1905, they had three young children: my uncle Richard King, 14; my mother Laura, 9; and my other uncle, Wendell, 4. Grandfather established two businesses: a wholesale grocery business, R.W. Smith and Co.; and later, Smith Brothers Realty. He was elected to serve in the Missouri General Assembly in 1922, representing the 4th District.

Chapter 1

My mother's parents, Richard and Kora Smith.

Dick on the tractor at our grandparents'
farm in Clay County.

The Stowers family homestead in Clay County.

After her family moved to Kansas City, my mother attended Hyde
Park Elementary School and graduated from Westport High School in 1915.
From there she went to the University of Missouri, where she graduated in
1921 with a Bachelor of Arts degree in English and Modern Languages.

Chapter 1

MY MOTHER'S INFLUENCE

When I was born on January 10, 1924, my mother nourished and tenderly cared for me, her first-born child. Two years later my brother, Richard West Stowers, was born. Mother, who had the primary responsibility of caring for Dick and me, would have done anything for us.

We enjoyed doing things with Mother. Jim played the saxophone, I played the clarinet and Mother played the piano.

On Sundays, the three of us walked to the Country Club Congregational Church where Jim sang in the choir.

On Easter in 1942, we were all baptized.

Dick Stowers

Mother taught us how to behave and instilled in us the values that have sustained us throughout our lives. We were loved and cherished. She encouraged us to treat others with courtesy, the same way we would like to be treated. I admired her tremendously and would have done anything for her, and I always did.

Mother was an extremely active person. Like her father, she was civic-minded and very involved in the community. She volunteered her talent and time to many medical organizations and auxiliaries, and she often served as president. She was also a great help to our father with his medical practice. She belonged to the American Association of University Women and for years was an active member of the Tri-Delta sorority. In 1976, she was the first to be honored by the sorority when she received the "Tri Delta of the Year" award for over fifty years service to the organization.

After my father died in 1945 at the age of 55, my mother decided to enter the business world. Like her father before her, she made a very successful career in the real estate business, retiring in 1978. She had a

Chapter 1

fantastic memory. She could drive up and down the streets of Kansas City and recall the exact amount for which each person had bought or sold their house. Amazingly, she also remembered the names of most of the people who owned those houses. She was an extremely determined person, starting to work early in the morning and continuing late into the night. Above all, she always treated people fairly.

After starting my own investment company, I wished I could have had a thousand sales people who worked as hard as she did. She was absolutely determined to do her very best. This trait of my mother's may be the reason that I am so persistent and determined.

Mother's wedding day, September 17, 1921.

Me, with my Mother and Dick.

Chapter 1

OUR FAMILY

When my parents first married, they lived in an apartment on Linwood Boulevard, a very pleasant neighborhood in Kansas City. Other members of my mother's family lived in the same building, including her parents, older brother, Richard King, and younger brother, Wendell, with his wife and daughter. Growing up so near our relatives was a great advantage for Dick and me and enabled us to enjoy the companionship of our cousin, Gwen. As we approached school age, Gwen's family moved to St. Joseph, Missouri, and we moved to a newer area in the southern part of the city.

Our new home, in the delightful, tree-lined neighborhood of Brookside, was within walking distance of our elementary school, our church and the shopping district. My brother, Dick, was my playmate and friend; but we also played with other children after school and belonged to a boys' club a few blocks from home.

It was a very enjoyable life. Dad was usually at home for breakfast before surgery. He would come home in the evening around 6 or 6:30, and we would all have dinner together. Mother cooked all of our meals. Our maid, Frieda Rolfe, lived on our third floor.

Our elementary school was just three blocks away from our home. After school we'd go play tennis. On rainy or cold days we would play hockey in the basement with a broom and a mop. One time when we were playing hockey, I accidentally bloodied Jim's upper eyelid with a bent screw hook on the end of the broom. You can still see the scar over his eye. We also played with the many children on the block.

Dick Stowers

Chapter 1

My parents cared about our happiness, but they also wanted to be proud of the way we conducted ourselves. Over time, I learned that if I did exactly what was expected of me, I would not get into trouble.

I hope that my mother and father would be proud of my brother and me and of our accomplishments. We were lucky to have had such wonderful parents. Their genes and the values which they passed on to us were the two most important things that made it possible for us to accomplish so much. They could not have given us a greater gift.

Me, with a patch on my right eye, and Dick, around 1934.

Dick and me a few years later.

Chapter 1

RICHARD KING SMITH
My Mother's Elder Brother

My mother's elder brother, Richard King Smith, was like a second father to me. After his father died in 1926, he took care of his mother for twenty years until her death in 1946. It was only then, at the age of 56, that he finally married.

Uncle King had a workshop with many kinds of tools, including large wood and metal lathes, drill presses, circular saws, band saws, jigsaws and a planer. I can vividly remember standing outside his workshop door when he said that if I was to come into his shop, I had to agree not to touch a thing unless he first gave me permission. Then I was free to walk around his shop holding my hands behind my back. Although I was extremely curious, I just looked and observed. I learned an important lesson: do not to take liberties with anything that is not mine, unless given permission to do so.

Uncle King and his wife, Olive.

Chapter 1

Me, with my saxophone.

One of my first experiences with Uncle King was learning how to wire a light fixture. I correctly wired a large Christmas light bulb to a plug, placed the electric plug in a socket, turned the switch on … and blew out the main fuse of the house. I quickly learned that the fuse had to be strong enough to handle all the current.

I was extremely inquisitive and eager to learn. So I was very fortunate to have an uncle who was mechanically inclined and also a great teacher. King had the time and the desire to help me learn about how things worked and how to fix them when they didn't.

In 1931, when I was 7 years old, King introduced me to his C Melody Saxophone to see if I might be interested in learning how to play that instrument. I was anxious to learn, but we soon found out that this particular model of saxophone was out of date. My father purchased for me the model that replaced it, the E flat Alto Saxophone. Over time, while practicing, I developed a keen appreciation for music. I was determined to be the best, so I practiced up to eight hours a day. In 1942, I won first place in the National Music Contest playing the Selmer Saxophone.

King truly enjoyed boating. Over the years he owned many boats. I remember the 30-foot homemade boat he had acquired called the Janice. Frankly, it truly looked homemade. It was made of thick wood and did not have very appealing lines. Regardless, it was fun to play on. We had many great times together on the Lake of the Ozarks in central Missouri.

Chapter 1

Uncle King's Janice, a 30-foot homemade, was safe and fun.

Later he traded the Janice for a 50 x 18 foot houseboat with a hull made of quarter-inch steel. It had steel casement windows and was a real home on the water. This boat was made by a steel tank company during the 1929 depression in an effort to keep people busy. Interestingly, the boat drew only eight inches of water. It could go anywhere.

There was a coal oil (kerosene) lantern on the Janice that produced so little light you could hardly read by it. I would have preferred a Coleman lantern that used gasoline, because it was five to ten times brighter than the old coal oil lamp. However, Uncle King was afraid that the Coleman lantern might explode and injure me, so he never purchased one.

We also had fun with a small outboard racing boat that had previously won a race on the Missouri River from St. Louis to Kansas City. He often

Chapter 1

gave visitors rough, short "joy" rides. Much later, when he moved to Florida, he bought a new 38-foot fiberglass cruiser which he used on the Intercoastal Waterway at Fort Lauderdale.

Uncle King and I had a wonderful relationship. We had the same interests. I still remember most of what he taught me. He encouraged me to be extremely accurate in whatever I did and to be proud of the results. The two of us spent many hours in his car driving back and forth to the Lake of the Ozarks to work on his boat. Those rides provided a marvelous opportunity for conversation. He was like a second father to me.

In 1956, I was 32 years old and had just started J. E. Stowers & Company – now called American Century Investments. I was concerned that others might consider me too young to be its president. With my Uncle King at the helm, the company would project an image of stability. For those reasons, I asked my Uncle King to be the President, a position he held for several years.

Sometime later, when my uncle felt extremely generous, he offered me $10,000. Today that would represent a gift of about $100,000. I certainly appreciated his offer. However, I told him there was absolutely no way I could possibly imagine all the things he must have done without in order to accumulate that sum. Although I was grateful, I had to refuse his gift because he might need it himself someday. However, I told him that I would feel extremely fortunate to receive a gift after he died. Soon after this, my uncle had a serious stroke and needed every dollar he had saved.

Chapter 1

What I Learned

Be proud of my family name.

Earn the respect of people.

Education is essential for future success.

Treat people as I would like to be treated.

Cultivate friendships and be loyal to family.

Do the best I can in whatever I choose to accomplish.

Know the value of money.

Take care of my appearance.

"The object is to develop in harmony
the physical, mental and moral powers,
not to make mere scholars
but to make men."

F.T. Kemper
Founder Kemper Military School

Chapter 2

Kemper Military School

―――

Chapter 2

KEMPER HONOR STANDARD

The Rules That All Kemper Live by ... Uphold ... and Enforce

I will tell the truth in all official statements.

That I will not cheat in recitations or examinations.

That I will not violate any pledge voluntarily given.

That I will never falsify any official papers or records.

That I will tolerate no violations thereof.

That I will support the honor commission in its administration of the standard.

Kemper Military School and College, the oldest military school west of the Mississippi, was founded in 1844.

Its primary goals were to provide an environment in which young men could learn self-discipline, time management, duty, academic excellence and leadership.

Just before and during my time at the school, there was a lot of new construction:

1937: a stadium and football fields
1939: an Academic Hall
1941: a Science Hall.

In 1942, there were nearly 600 cadets, an unprecedented number of young men.

Chapter 2

Our family at Kemper with Dick and me in uniform.

Chapter 2

CHALLENGE OF KEMPER MILITARY SCHOOL

In 1938, my father was convinced that our country would go to war. He wanted me to enter the service as an officer rather than as an enlisted man. So when I was fourteen, my parents enrolled me in Kemper Military School as a second-year high school student. At that time, eighty percent of the students were of junior college age. I was one of the youngest and felt challenged by the older cadets to rise to a higher standard. I was forced to mature in a hurry. My age was evident to everyone because of the star on my door indicating that no one was permitted to smoke in my room.

I was determined to succeed and worked very, very hard in all the activities available at Kemper. I ended up being a member of all four of the honor societies, as well as a member of the Rifle Team.

I was not the first man in my family to be an expert marksman. My great, great grandfather was nicknamed "Chief" Stowers. My Dad told me a story of this ancestor from the backwoods of Kentucky:

RIFLEMEN PLACE HIGH IN HEARST MATCHES

The results of the National R.O.T.C. Rifle Competition for the William Randolf Hearst Trophies for 1941 have recently been announced.

Continuing their traditional habit of placing in this group, Sgt. G. J. Kerr's first Kemper team, composed of J.I. Amos, R.F. Jann, J.E. Stowers, F.C. Caldwell, and M.C. Beekman, placed second among essentially Military Schools with a score of 909 followed closely by Kemper's second team composed of D. J. Barr, G. C. Gerger, G. M. Kirkpatrick, N. W. Beach, and H. B. Hindson with a score of 905.

The essentially Military Schools were topped by St. Thomas Military Academy's high score of 917 with individual honors also taken by a score 193.

Because of his great marksmanship, your great, great grandfather was known as "Chief" Stowers back in the pioneer days. When he turned 83, he went out hunting to demonstrate to the younger generation that he was still as skillful as ever. That day he shot a squirrel, a fox and a brace of quail.

Chapter 2

My Dad was also a championship marksman who, at the age of 20, represented the Missouri National Guard in a national rifle contest at Camp Perry.

DETERMINED TO BE THE VERY BEST

While I was at Kemper, I continued to practice my saxophone. When I went home to Kansas City on breaks, I would visit my music teacher for new assignments. I was still determined to become one of the best saxophone players in the country.

Being prepared paid off when I entered the National Music Competition in 1941. I won first place in the saxophone competition.

To fill in the time while waiting to see if I would be chosen to play in the concert band, I began to practice my saxophone. The man next to me asked why I wasn't up there getting ready with the others. I answered that I had not been invited.

He said, "Well, you are now." He happened to be the Concert Band conductor!

My determination had paid off. Not only did I win first place in the saxophone competition, I also got to play in the National Band Concert with all the best players.

> Saturday Evening, May 10, 1941
>
> **2,300 Musicians Compete in Final Day's Contests**
>
> Bands, Orchestras and Soloists at Festival's Wind-up
>
> **ALTO SAXOPHONE**
>
> Minor M. Love, Radium, Kan.; George Sherman, Salina, Kan.; J. E. Stowers, Kemper Military Academy, Boonville, Mo.; Millard Pope, Platte City, Mo.; Causby Cole, Raytown, Mo.

My hard work at Kemper paid off in other ways as well. In my fourth year at Kemper, I earned the privilege of becoming a cadet officer on the Corps Staff. This honor came with several great benefits and the opportunity to take on the responsibility of being a student leader.

Chapter 2

JOINING THE SCHOLASTIC HONOR SOCIETY

There was a particular cadet in my class who stood out scholastically. His excellent grades seemed to come effortlessly. I wondered about what I would have to do to excel. I was absolutely determined to reach the top of my class. I realized that in order to achieve my goal, I would absolutely have to try much harder than that cadet.

To start with, I would have to concentrate on trying to teach myself how to learn. Facts alone did not make much sense to me. Even though I was able to memorize important isolated facts, they would gradually fade from my memory. What could I do to improve my retention?

Why should I clutter up my mind with isolated facts? I needed to understand *why* it was important to remember a particular fact. I am extremely curious about how things work and why they work. If I know the *why* associated with a particular fact, it is easier for me to remember that fact forever.

I found that if I truly did not understand something, I had not thought about it long enough. In that case, I would dig in and try harder to understand the reasoning behind that fact. This is how I was able to accumulate knowledge. Following this process helped me to challenge myself to do more than I thought I was capable of doing.

THE BLIND DATE BUREAU

As a cadet officer, one of my most enjoyable duties was to be in charge of the Blind Date Bureau, arranging dates for the cadets with girls who attended Stephens and Christian Colleges in Columbia, Missouri. Sometimes a big name orchestra would play for us.

As the officer in charge of the Blind Date Bureau, I would get together ahead of time with the girls from Stephens and Christian Colleges

Chapter 2

who coordinated their Blind Date Bureaus. We had fun trying to match the cadets and girls with suitable dance partners. I said to the girls, "If you are straight with me, I'll be straight with you." I would select a cadet and describe him as honestly as I could. Then my counterpart would pick a girl they thought would be suitable for my candidate. For example, we might match two people who were known as wallflowers. It usually turned out pretty well.

PROGRAM DANCES – KEMPER STYLE

The way Kemper organized its program dances was a fantastic idea. A few days before the dance, the cadets would take their program card and write their name on the four required spots: first dance, the two dances around intermission and the last dance. Then we would go around and fill the rest of our dance card with the names of our cadet friends.

The night of the dance, we would dance the first dance with our date, then look for the friend whose name was listed for the second dance. We would exchange partners.

At the end of the second dance, we would repeat the process and so on, all evening long.

This gave everyone a chance to dance with a variety of partners. It was a lot of fun for both the cadets and the girls.

Even when I had a girlfriend, I really enjoyed dancing with other girls, and I still got to be with my girlfriend for the four important dances.

The girls would arrive in five, six or seven busses. Each cadet knew the name of his date ahead of time. I would line up the boys, each one clutching an orchid corsage, to welcome their future partners as they came off the busses. I already had a list of the girls' names and, as I called each one, I would invite her escort to meet his date.

Chapter 2

Candid humor about me, the officer in charge of the Blind Date Bureau.

As a perfect gentleman, he was expected to dance the programmed dances with his partner then escort her safely back to the bus at the end of the evening. It was a good system. Almost everyone met someone they really liked and had a good time.

WHAT OTHERS THINK ABOUT ME CAN MAKE A DIFFERENCE

Officers from the regular army would occasionally come to Kemper for an official military inspection. Part of the inspection involved the visiting officers testing the cadets on different military subjects. We sat in rows and the officers asked us questions one after another.

Chapter 2

I remember my last year at Kemper, when I was in a group being tested by some regular army men. An officer asked the cadet beside me, "Describe a member of the forward echelon." The cadet named a member of the rear echelon, not the forward echelon. The officer accepted his answer.

The cadet had misunderstood the question. After the officer accepted the cadet's answer, he turned to me and asked for another person in that echelon. I was in a pickle.

Should I describe another person in the *rear* echelon so as not to show up the other cadet, or should I answer the original question about the *forward* echelon that the officer had asked and show up the officer who did not catch the error? I decided to ask the officer to please repeat the question.

Later my classmates taunted me, saying, "You did not pay attention!"

I got fed up and defensively blurted out, "I don't give a damn what you think!"

What a mistake! Some of these cadets quoted me out of context and passed on to others that "Jim Stowers doesn't give a damn." This statement eventually reached the ears of the head of the military department. "Mr. Stowers doesn't give a damn."

The reputation I had so carefully built over four years was shot with one careless comment.

I learned the hard way to be more careful of what I say. In particular, I learned not to say, "I don't give a damn." I absolutely do care about what others think of me.

Chapter 2

My proud father shaking hands with me at Kemper.

Chapter 2

What I Learned

To grow up in a hurry and rise to a higher standard.

To take orders before I gave them.
- *The meaning and purpose behind authority.*
- *My life and the lives of others could depend on my following orders.*

To treat others the way I would like to be treated.
- *You never forget being treated unfairly.*

Never ask someone to do something that I would not be willing to do myself.
- *If I wanted to be a leader, how could I expect others to do something I was not willing to do?*

I cannot do everything myself.
- *I might be an expert at some things, but not at everything.*
- *I could not win a war entirely by myself.*

Always tell the truth.
- *How can anyone trust or rely on what I say if I am not truthful?*

To rely on what others in authority say.
- *I must trust my superiors.*

I had to work to earn the respect and confidence of others.
- *Respect cannot be given to just anyone; it must be earned over time.*

Try to be an example that others would like to follow.
- *Take pride in what I do and in what I believe.*
- *Try my very best at whatever I choose to do.*
- *Become a worthy model for others to follow.*

It takes a long time to build a reputation and a moment of carelessness to lose it.

I truly care about what others think about me.

Chapter 3

Pilot Training

Chapter 3

PILOT TRAINING

My father was right when, in 1938, he anticipated that our country would go to war. Three years later, on December 7, 1941, Japan bombed Pearl Harbor and we were at war.

By the following June, I had completed four years of infantry ROTC at Kemper Military School qualifying for a commission as a second lieutenant in the infantry. I declined to accept my commission because I was deferred from military service as a pre-medical student. My father and grandfather were both surgeons, and I had hoped to follow the family tradition.

I began pre-medical studies at the University of Missouri in the fall of 1942. In order to maintain my pre-med deferral, the government required me to have a monthly physical exam. It was annoying to take time out from my studies to do this every month. Since I would probably not be able to enter medical school for two more years, I felt it would be more patriotic to enter the military and finish my medical studies after the war.

When I was at Kemper, I became convinced that the infantry was not for me. So I asked the recruiter if the Army could assure me that if I accepted the commission of second lieutenant in the infantry, it would transfer me to the Army Air Corps. The officer said he would try, but could not guarantee it. Because I liked the glory and fascination of flying, the uncertainty of that answer was not acceptable to me. I immediately drove up to Fort Leavenworth, Kansas, and enlisted as a private in the Army Air Corps.

Chapter 3

Me, age 21, in my favorite casual attire.

Chapter 3

KEESLER FIELD – BASIC TRAINING

In December 1943, I reported to Keesler Field in Biloxi, Mississippi, for Basic Training. This is where everyone was introduced to the basics of being in the Army Air Corps. At first, we slept on a cot in a tent and endured the cold. Later we were moved into barracks. We learned how to march in formation, the use of arms, self-defense, teamwork and above all, discipline and how to follow orders.

The physical rigors of basic training were followed by other kinds of challenges. We were subjected to some amazing mental and physical tests developed to determine our aptitude for flying. For example, wc were tested to see if we could perform different tasks with each hand at the same time.

One test I particularly remember involved a pegboard with square holes. There were square pegs with round tops painted half in blue and half in yellow.

Becoming an Air Corps Pilot

1943 *Basic Training*
Keesler Field, Biloxi, MS

1944 *College Training Detachment* (CTD)
Middle State College, Murfreesboro, TN

Pre-Flight Training
Maxwell Field, AL

Primary Flight Training
Decatur, AL

Basic Flight Training
Stewart Field, West Point, Newburg, NY

1945 *Advanced Flight Training*
Napier Field, Dothan, AL

April 1945, received Pilot Wings and rank of 2nd Lieutenant

Fighter Gunnery Instructor's School
Victoria, TX

October 1945, discharged from Air Corps

Chapter 3

Image courtesy John Allan - Aylsham, England

Aeronca 7AC

Our task was to see how many of these square pegs could be removed, turned 180 degrees, and then be reinserted back into the square holes. I had no trouble with any of the tests. I actually found them an interesting challenge.

COLLEGE TRAINING DETACHMENT (CTD)

My next step after completing Basic Training in December of 1943, was to attend, for six months, the "College Training Detachment" (CTD) at Middle State College in Murfreesboro, Tennessee. Even though I had already completed two years of college, I had not yet studied navigation. We also had an introduction to flying which consisted of spending 10 hours of flying time in a small Aeronca plane. The purpose seemed to be to test how well we could physically tolerate being airborne.

Chapter 3

DOING MORE THAN I THINK I CAN

The Army Air Corps tried to convince its officers and airmen that they could always do much more than they thought they could. One particular incident, which I will never forget, took place late one afternoon after a physical training session. The instructor spoke to the squadron:

"As you all know, we have had a great deal of bad weather for the past weeks. This has prevented you from performing certain exercises, which would have helped condition you for this new exercise. Today the schedule calls for us to run around a 440-yard track 20 times in formation.

We realize this may be difficult for you. However, the schedule calls for us to do it and we must. We will proceed to jog around the track in formation. If anyone should voluntarily drop out, that person will immediately be sent to the flight surgeon for a thorough physical examination. On the other hand, if anyone should involuntarily drop out, nothing will be done."

It seemed absolutely impossible for me to run around a 440-yard track 20 times. In fact, I wasn't sure I could run around the track even once, especially since we were wearing heavy army boots. Though very few of us believed we could accomplish this goal, we had no choice but to start running. Frankly, I was surprised to make it around the first lap which didn't seem too bad considering how many more laps we had yet to run.

We tried everything to keep our minds off of our sore feet. We kidded each other about who was going to drop out and who could run the distance. When we finished the second lap, I was even more surprised that I completed it.

We kept running in formation, completing one lap after another; but the goal of 20 laps seemed an impossibility. By the end of the eleventh lap, only one man in our squadron had dropped out. Since he did this voluntarily, he was immediately sent to the flight surgeon's office. No one else wanted to see the flight surgeon, so we kept running.

By the end of the fourteenth lap, most of the men were quiet. There was no more kidding. Everyone was concentrating on trying to accomplish this daunting challenge. This was not a competition; we were intensely focused on surviving this ordeal together. As each lap went by, we were concerned that we might not make it through the next one; yet somehow, we did.

Finally, to our amazement, we completed the last lap. We accomplished more than we thought possible. Three men in the squadron dropped out voluntarily. They were sent to see the flight surgeon and were not seen again. Not one man fell out unconscious.

The Air Corps absolutely proved to me that I can always do more than I think I can.

PRE-FLIGHT TRAINING
MAXWELL FIELD, ALABAMA

Having overcome the hurdle of being airborne, we were now faced with learning the fundamentals of flying and all of the practical knowledge required to navigate a plane safely, such as the theory of flight, communications, weather and aircraft and ship identification.

Being a new cadet at Kemper had been rough, but that was nothing compared with what it was like to be in Pre-Flight Training. In my unit, many more young men wanted to be pilots than were needed. They were washing men out of training every night for the slightest reasons, sometimes unrelated to competence.

Chapter 3

I was determined that I *would* survive, but how? The strategy I used was to avoid drawing any attention to myself. During the first four weeks, I tried not to stand out in any way. The most important thing was to follow all the rules without drawing the attention of the other cadets. My plan was to:

Make no friends, but be polite.

Try not to stand out in any way.

Be by myself.

I'm naturally outgoing, so keeping a low profile was extremely difficult for me. However, my determination to remain invisible paid off the day we qualified as upper classmen. While we stood at attention in formation we were told, "Anyone interested in trying out for the Corps staff, please take one step forward."

I took that step. Everyone looked surprised. Who was this guy? No one recognized me. My strategy had worked. From a pool of 20,000 cadets, I was chosen to be on the Corps staff as Corps Supply Officer with the rank of Cadet Captain.

BE DETERMINED

If I had been washed out of pilot training because I was unable to meet any of the challenges, I would have been sent to Fort Benning as a second lieutenant in the infantry. Since my passion was to be a pilot, that would have been devastating to me.

One of the first tests we faced in pre-flight training was an obstacle course called the Burma Road. The objective was to reach the end of the

Chapter 3

course before the instructor. Cadets who failed were sent to the hospital for a physical exam, after which they would most likely be washed out of the Corps.

One of the obstacles was a 10-12 foot high wall. You had to go over the wall, not around it. How on earth could anyone get over that wall? The answer was simple, *stand back and run over it.* This was new to me; it represented a physical impossibility. However, I was absolutely determined not to be washed out. The alternative spurred me to overcome this challenge and not let it stand in the way of my becoming a pilot.

The wall loomed in the distance like a fortress. I gathered my strength and, without flinching from my determination, ran faster and faster until suddenly I was over the wall. How did it happen? It was simple, really. I ran one or two steps up the wall, grabbed the top of the wall and pulled myself over.

My determination boosted my confidence, enabling me to accomplish what appeared to be an impossible task.

PRIMARY FLIGHT TRAINING

My rigorous preparation was finally rewarded. I was sent to Decatur, Alabama, for Primary Flight Training where I flew the PT-17. There were hundreds of those planes there, with a 300 hp engine, two sets of wings and a top speed of 80 miles an hour. Many of these planes are seen today on the coasts pulling advertisements.

Chapter 3

Image courtesy Defense Visual Information Center.

151 Boeing PT-17

The training in Decatur was broken into three parts:

The theory of flight

navigation

Understanding aircraft

aircraft engines

Learning how to fly

how to take off and land

link trainer instrument flying

acrobatics

I finally completed all the preliminaries and was ready for the next step. A fellow cadet, Jack Urie, informed me that there were a few openings in the next class for Basic Flight Training at Stewart Field in New York

Chapter 3

where the West Point cadets fly from in the summer. Jack was excited about the chance to go to West Point and asked if I would like to apply with him. I answered, "Yes," but also reminded him that it would probably be extremely strict training. We applied in November 1944. Both of us were selected.

BASIC FLIGHT TRAINING

At Stewart Field, we became the first class to fly the amazing North American AT-6. The engine had about 600 horsepower. It was an all-metal plane that flew around 160 miles an hour. The plane had many more dials on the instrument panel than the PT-17.

One particular challenge was to learn to fly in winter. One of the pilot instructors, a combat veteran, told us that the winter at Stewart was worse than the weather he had experienced in combat.

North American AT-6

Chapter 3

Beyond the challenges of flying a larger, more powerful plane and the difficult weather conditions, our training at Stewart Field included more acrobatics, flying in formation and learning to land on ice.

A SURVIVOR STRATEGY THAT CHANGED MY WAY OF THINKING

During our time at Stewart Field, one of the fighter pilots who had survived combat was reassigned to our pilot training. He shared a strategy that became a tool I have used throughout my life when I am faced with a problem.

He suggested that pilots going into combat should determine **ahead of time** which evasive maneuvers they should execute to survive an enemy attack. He indicated that waiting to decide which evasive action to take until you are actually faced with the enemy, takes time that might result in being shot down and losing your life.

"If you want to improve your chances of surviving in combat," he said, "why not try to eliminate the time required to decide what maneuver to perform? The way to do that is to sit down right now and determine exactly what you would do in every possible enemy attack."

That suggestion immediately got my attention. To counter a particular attack, I would have to decide, in advance, all the evasive maneuvers possible and then determine which evasive action would be the best.

For days, I spent my open hours planning evasive actions for various situations. Which maneuvers would be hardest for an enemy pilot to counter? There were so many ways the enemy could attack … knowing the best evasive action could enable me to survive.

Chapter 3

I further refined my thinking by imagining which maneuvers the enemy pilot might expect me to execute during his attack. Would his conclusion change my response? I was finally convinced that if I had to go into combat, I would be prepared to anticipate the enemy maneuvers and would survive.

My two years of pilot training taught me lessons that I still use in my daily life. I often remember this survival strategy that I learned at Stewart Field. Before I commit to a plan, I look at all the problems that could come up and devise ways to overcome them. My plans go a lot more smoothly when I take the time to do this.

MOVING ON

Before going to Stewart Field, I was convinced that the discipline there would be truly *chicken*, because it was associated with West Point. I was surprised, because I never had such a wonderful time. It was the best country club I had ever attended. Why did I think this was the case?

Chicken: A 1941 slang term meaning to be insistent on petty details of duty or discipline.

Since Stewart had a reputation for being extremely strict, only those who welcomed that type of discipline applied. As a result, everyone lived up to what was expected of him, and we all had a fantastic time. I learned a great lesson: if you live up to what is expected of you, you are not likely to get into trouble.

It was time for us to move on to more advanced training. Would I be assigned to fly bombers or fighters? Here is Jack Urie's description of the "scientific" way they chose our assignments:

Chapter 3

We completed our basic Flight Training at Stewart Field at West Point. They lined us all up on the side of the building by height. They wanted the tallest guy to the right and the shortest guy to the left. We juggled ourselves so that we were in this line by height. When we got there, I was 6'1" and Jim was 6'.

They asked, "Well, where is the guy who is exactly 6' tall? Jim was exactly 6', so he put up his hand.

They said, "OK, all you guys on the left, the shorter ones, go to fighter school. All of you guys on the right, who are taller, go to bomber school."

That was the way they selected us.

Jim asked, "Where do I go?"

The answer was, "You have your choice. You can go either to fighter school or to bomber school."

ADVANCED FLIGHT TRAINING
NAPIER FIELD

Flying a bomber is like driving a bus. On the other hand, it is an exciting challenge for a fighter pilot when he uses all his reflexes and knowledge to maneuver a plane so he can survive. I decided that I wanted to be a fighter pilot, so the Air Corps transferred me to Napier Field in Dothan, Alabama, for Advanced Flight Training. To my disappointment, I once again had to fly the familiar North American AT-6. But it wasn't as easy as I had assumed, because planes fly differently in warm weather.

Chapter 3

A Bird Can Fly Better

One evening, I was practicing night landings. On one of the approaches, as my plane was about 10 feet above the runway, the plane started to snap roll, which means it started to roll rapidly over onto its back. I was extremely fortunate to have been alert at that time and ready to immediately apply the correct rudder control which prevented the plane from landing upside down. This fast reaction probably saved my life.

This event seriously concerned me. What on earth could I do in the future to prevent my over-confidence from hurting me? What could I do to convince myself to remain alert?

For the rest of the time I spent in the Air Force and the ten years I flew the company jets, I was absolutely determined to say, just before making my take-off roll, *"Remember, Jim, a bird can fly better than you can."*

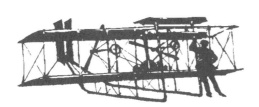

It won't fly, Orville

Chapter 3

A Close Call

The day before I was to graduate, the Army Air Corps realized that our class had not performed a low level cross-country flight. We had to put our flight suits back on and take the cross-country. Our task was to fly as fast and low as we could, not over 500 feet above the ground. During the flight, my engine suddenly quit. I was forced to make an emergency belly landing between trees in an isolated field. I was sure that I would be washed out because of pilot error. Instead, I was surprised to learn that the Air Corps had determined that my plane's engine had a serious mechanical malfunction.

I finally graduated and received my wings in April 1945, with a promotion to Second Lieutenant pilot.

Fighter Gunnery Training

Although the war in Europe ended in the spring of 1945, we were still fighting in the Pacific. I continued my training, this time in aircraft gunnery. At first, I flew AT-6's out of Eglin Air Force base in Florida and practiced aircraft gunnery over the Gulf of Mexico. I was proud to have twice shot down the banner pulled by the tow plane.

When I completed gunnery school at Eglin, I went back to Napier Field in Alabama to check out in the Curtis Wright P-40 fighter. These were the planes flown by the Flying Tigers.

Chapter 3

Sadly for my flying career, it became clear that the Air Corps had too many pilots. As a result, they restricted our flying hours and began to have pilots do maintenance on the planes.

To further my training, I went to headquarters and asked if there were any openings in the instrument flight school. That school did not have any openings. However, I learned there was an opening in fighter gunnery school. This was an opportunity I could not pass up. So in August of 1945, I signed up and was transferred to fighter gunnery instructor school at Foster Field in Victoria, Texas.

Once again, I was flying the faithful AT-6. They were also flying the P-51 and the P-47 there. It was too early for the jet. Each day we flew from Foster Field down to Matagorda Island off the Gulf Coast for our gunnery practice. The temperature was so hot down on the gulf that we had to wear leather gloves to protect our hands while we were flying.

Image courtesy National Museum of the USAF.

P-40

Chapter 3

Image courtesy National Museum of the USAF.

B-26. I flew this in the Reserves.

MY FLYING ADVENTURES CONTINUE

The first atomic bomb was dropped on Japan, August 6, 1945. Shortly after that, the war was over. When I indicated that I wanted out of the service to continue my medical education, I was immediately "assigned" to play volleyball while waiting to be transferred back to my previous base.

Finally, on October 22, 1945, I was discharged from the Army Air Corps, which later became the U.S. Air Force.

Because of my love of flying, I joined the Air Force Reserve and flew from Fairfax Field in Kansas City, Kansas. I checked out and flew the AT-6, C-45, AT-11 and the B-26. Later, my Reserve Unit was transferred to Richards Gebauer Field south of Kansas City, Missouri.

In 1956, I went back on active duty for a few weeks to learn to fly jets. I was stationed with the Air Force Jet Transition School at Craig Field in Selma, Alabama. I checked out in the T-33 single engine jet. It was incredible to fly a jet.

Chapter 3

LEARNING FROM MISTAKES

One winter, I was flying an AT-6 Air Force airplane from Kansas City to Chicago. It was midnight. I was alone in the plane and having trouble staying awake. To wake myself up, I tried all kinds of things including pinching myself. Nothing seemed to work.

I decided to open the canopy, hoping the cool breezes would revive me, but that didn't help very much. This really worried me because I was getting increasingly tired. I decided to put my head out into the slipstream to see if that would revive me. It was cold out there, but even that did not make me more alert. For some reason, it occurred to me to turn my head and look back at the tail of the airplane. As I turned, my goggles went clear out about three feet, stretching the rubber band. I instantly thought, "My gosh! When they come back, it's going to really hurt!" Sure enough, when I pulled my head back, the goggles suddenly snapped back, hitting me hard on the head. That really woke me up! From then on, I did not fly unless I was fully rested.

T-33

Chapter 3

CONCLUSION

I was most fortunate to have had a variety of experiences flying everything from propeller planes to single engine fighters. As flight technology advanced, I kept up my flying skills and flew the company jet for many years. Although I have bridged three generations in the progress of flight, I can close my eyes and still re-live the sensation I had in the open cockpit wearing my goggles and helmet.

WHAT I LEARNED

You can absolutely do more than you think you can.

Do your very best at whatever you choose to do.

Whatever you do, try to know more about it than anyone else.

Think about the consequences of your actions and plan ahead before making a decision.

Keeping a low profile can sometimes be an advantage in meeting your goals.

It is important not to let over-confidence undermine your ability to constantly remain alert.

Remember, a bird can fly better than you can.

Chapter 4

Medical School

Me, on my trusty motor scooter in Iowa.

Chapter 4

MEDICAL SCHOOL IN MISSOURI

Imagine a young man encouraged by his parents to be the best he can be. Now imagine the same young man eager to become a doctor and follow the family tradition laid down by his father and grandfather. In October 1945, with the war over, I was discharged as a pilot from the Air Corps. I re-enrolled at the University of Missouri in January 1946, to continue my education in my other love, medicine.

It was a sad time in my life. My father, role model and hero, had died suddenly only six months before, leaving me emotionally unprepared. I became even more determined to emulate this man I loved and follow in the family tradition of becoming a doctor.

A COMMENT THAT CHANGED MY LIFE

One of the most memorable courses I elected to take when I first returned to my premed studies was cellular physiology. The biological study of the function of living organisms and their parts was taught by Dr. Daniel Mazia, head of research for the university.

Dr. Mazia was an amazing teacher who was able to make science courses come alive. I studied extremely hard and was absolutely determined to convince him that I truly understood his subject. On one particular essay exam, I wrote countless pages in answer to the questions. When the graded papers were returned, I was disappointed that I received only a B+ followed by the comment, **"I have never seen so much information unorganized."**

This shocked me into thinking that I must always take time to sort out my thoughts before expressing them. I was truly grateful for that criticism. It changed my life. I was determined to organize my thinking so that no one would ever have the chance to say that of me again.

Chapter 4

I had an excellent rapport with Dr. Mazia. He tried to entice me into becoming a research scientist. I was flattered by the thought, but I was determined to become a doctor like my father.

I was deeply touched by Dr. Mazia's death.

Dr. Mazia became an eminent biologist who inspired generations of cell biologists. He died June 9, 1996, at the age of 83. He was a member of both the National Academy of Sciences and the American Academy of Arts and Sciences.

In April of 2000, after learning that Dr. Mazia had died, I sent a check in his memory to the Stanford University-Mazia Lectureship Fund.

WORK HARD, PLAY HARD

I had discovered something in flight training: when you work, why not work hard? But since it is just as important to have fun, when you play, why not play hard? Putting your all into whatever you do is all that can be expected of you.

When I entered medical school at the University of Missouri, my brother and I lived together. I had a motor scooter he was welcome to borrow. The girls at Christian and Stephens Colleges were not allowed to go on dates in cars, even if there was a formal dance. So we'd go over on our motor scooter to meet them. Then we'd all walk to the dance in our fancy clothes.

Jim and I were together for awhile in Columbia. We used to double date.

I remember a funny event. One time, we were at a show with our dates. Jim's pathology professor was sitting behind us. He leaned over and said to Jim, "What are you doing here?"

Jim turned around and said, "Saturday night's my night to howl, Doctor."

Dick Stowers

Chapter 4

MEDICAL SCHOOL IN IOWA

Since the University of Missouri only offered the first two years of medical school, I went on to the University of Iowa for my third and fourth years of medical education.

Just as in the Air Corps, medical schools eliminated many people, often for insignificant reasons. Fifty people began medical school with me in Missouri, but only eighteen of us graduated with a bachelor's degree in medicine.

At Iowa, I was determined to survive and remain in medical school.

LOOKING THE PART WITH MOTOR SCOOTERS AND A MERCURY CONVERTIBLE

At the medical school at the University of Iowa, parking around the campus was at a premium. If I had driven a car, I would have had to park blocks away. Instead I decided to use my bright red motor scooter for transportation so that I could drive straight up to the front door of the building where my class was held. When it rained, of course, I got wet; when it snowed, I got cold. But it was convenient and extremely inexpensive to operate.

1951. Mother, in my Mercury convertible in California on the way to the Air Force base where I was a doctor for the summer.

Chapter 4

Most of the medical students and residents used old cars; some even drove old Model A Fords. I was the rare one who drove a motor scooter. Some doctors quietly suggested that I was tarnishing the image of the medical profession by riding a motor scooter back and forth to class.

That comment irritated me. So on a cold day in December, I went down to the local Mercury dealer and traded my motor scooter for a brand new, white, 1949 Mercury convertible. The dealer gave me $500 credit for my motor scooter, and I added $2,000 from government bonds I bought during World War II.

By driving the convertible around the city, I no longer tarnished the medical profession's image, but I probably made some of the doctors and medical students envious.

I seriously question whether this action helped me improve my relationships with others.

FIGHT ONE MORE ROUND

One challenge during my third year was a psychology exam that, in my opinion, was poorly written. It was a True and False test where the examiner used words such as *always* and *never*. Well, things are rarely *always* or *never*, so every time I saw those words in a question, I circled false. I was upset when I failed the test. I went to see the professor and asked him for an explanation. He said that I did not answer the questions correctly. I replied, "Nothing is ever always or never."

"But you know what I mean," he said.

I stood my ground. "I certainly do not. You said *always* and I circled *false* which, in my mind, is the correct answer."

Chapter 4

That was apparently the wrong thing to say. Because I stood my ground with the professor, I failed the psychology course and had to repeat the entire year. However, I wasn't going to let this decision discourage me from becoming a doctor, so I repeated that whole third year of medicine.

WRONG DIAGNOSIS, DOCTOR

At that time, in medical circles there was an old rivalry between the internal medicine doctors and the surgeons. The internists accused the surgeons of being knife happy, implying that they wanted to take a peek inside a body in order to learn what was wrong with a patient. The internists, on the other hand, wanted to diagnose and treat a patient without using the knife. Surgery for them was a last resort. For the surgeons, of course, cutting out the diseased part was the method of choice – get rid of the cause and the patient would be cured.

A few weeks before the end of my final semester of my second attempt at third year medicine, I got caught in the politics of the internist/surgeon battle.

One evening, I had a terrible pain in my stomach. I did what I was supposed to do and reported to an internal medicine doctor at his office in the hospital. The doctor examined me and said there were three possible diagnoses. I don't recall the first two, but the third was that the pain was psychosomatic. I was told to go home.

During the night, my pain became extreme. Early the next morning, I rushed to the emergency room. A chest surgeon, who was one of my teachers, was on call. He asked me some questions and inquired about the internist's diagnosis. He then did a careful and thorough physical exam. "Jim, you have acute appendicitis and need to be operated on immediately," he declared. I agreed to the operation, providing that he would perform the surgery. A chest surgeon performing an appendectomy?!

Chapter 5

Looking Toward the Future

Mother, my first business mentor.

Chapter 5

MISFORTUNE TURNS INTO GOOD FORTUNE

Despite the unfairness at the University of Iowa, I tried to salvage my medical career. I went to Research Hospital in Kansas City, where I was permitted to work as an extern while trying to determine how to get back into medicine.

If you want to succeed, you should strike out on new paths rather than travel the worn paths of accepted success.

John D. Rockefeller, JR.

The incident at the medical school in Iowa meant I would be blackballed at every medical school in the United States. If I wanted to stay in the profession, the only avenue open to me was to go abroad.

Looking back, it is extremely fortunate that this event happened. While working very hard in medical school, I sometimes thought to myself that if I worked as hard at just about anything else, I might be more successful and happier.

If the incident had not happened, I question whether I would have voluntarily walked away from the field of medicine. I am confident that I would have helped people by being an excellent doctor, but it is highly unlikely that I would have been able to do all the other things I have done in my life. Since Virginia did not intend to marry a doctor, I might not have been able to persuade her to be my wife.

Chapter 5

GETTING TO KNOW MYSELF

My military experience taught me to thoroughly analyze a situation before making a decision about which direction to take. It was time to evaluate my personal strengths and weaknesses. In other words, it was time to do some soul searching. I asked myself:

What are my personal strengths and weaknesses?

What do I love to do?

What are my traits and attitudes?

What must I do in order to achieve success?

What must I do to avoid premature death?

Do I truly need people in my life?

Do I believe that I can enjoy life without people?

Who will take care of me in a time of financial need?

Lord! We know what we are,

but know not what we may be.

From *Hamlet* By William Shakespeare

Chapter 5

WHAT ARE MY PERSONAL STRENGTHS AND WEAKNESSES?

Education. My strengths lay in medical training, flight training and musical education. Some of the courses I studied which could help me determine which direction I should take were: mathematics, inorganic and organic chemistry, physics, economics, business law and geology.

In medical school, beyond the science and technique of medicine, I learned first-hand how to treat people courteously, how to develop rapport and how to gain the confidence and trust of others.

My Appearance. Overall, this was one of my strengths. I was tall, slim, attractive and appropriately dressed. I had an erect posture and above all, wore a friendly smile.

Life Experiences. After many hours of practicing the saxophone, I became an expert with that instrument. From my Uncle King, I learned how things work and how to fix them. I spent several summers on a farm where I learned a little about farm work and a lot about life. However, I had never really earned a living, except for my time in the Air Force and one summer, between my 3rd and 4th year of medicine, when I acted as a flight surgeon and even delivered babies.

Chapter 5

What Do I Love?

One of my loves was flying airplanes, especially jets. However, I did not believe flying represented a challenging career for me. Another love was listening to good music. I enjoyed figure skating and ballroom dancing because they enabled me to express my inner feelings. These would probably not help me in a new career.

What are My Traits and Attitudes?

The traits which I regarded, and still regard, as my most treasured qualities are that I am gregarious, honest and trustworthy. Close behind those traits is sincerity; I always try to "speak from the heart." I am also absolutely determined, courteous, dependable and consistent.

I am a logical thinker and a perfectionist.

I am proud, sentimental and extremely passionate about my beliefs.

I recognize that I do not know all the answers, and that I absolutely need the help of others.

My attitude is positive. I am happy, enthusiastic, optimistic and romantic. I am caring and quite sensitive to the feelings of others. I am serious about what I say, but do not take myself seriously.

I aspire to have good health, be accepted by others, maintain an image others expect, be an inspiration, be fair in my dealings, be considerate, be open minded, be the best I can be, be successful and be remembered for what I have done for others, rather than for what I have done for myself.

My wish for others is that they feel loved, respected and trusted by me. I desire that people be sinccre with me and speak from the heart.

Chapter 5

WHAT MUST I DO IN ORDER TO BECOME A SUCCESS?

I knew I was a good pilot. I also had enough experience in medicine to feel I could be an outstanding doctor. I analyzed the traits that helped me become successful in these areas and listed others I needed to acquire.

The secret in business is to know something that nobody else knows.
Aristotle Onassis

To be a success, I needed to know more than others; work harder and longer; and treat others the way I wanted to be treated. In addition, I had to admit that I did not know all the answers and that I needed all the help that I could get.

I had to strive for success and not attempt to do anything unless I was absolutely determined to do my very best. I had to truly believe that "The Best is Yet to Be."

WHAT MUST I DO TO AVOID A PREMATURE DEATH?

After my father died of a heart attack, I learned that he had poor circulation that prevented the blood from flowing freely in his legs. There may have been many reasons for this condition – two of which were that my father did not exercise, and he was a chain smoker. What, then, did I need to do to avoid a premature death?

I believed that the primary reason for all the calcium buildup in my father's legs was his inactivity. He just did not exercise his legs enough. I reasoned that in order to extend my life span, I would have to exercise.

96

Chapter 5

With determination, I set up an exercise regimen to challenge my cardiovascular system and strengthen the rest of my body with isometric exercises. The most important of all my exercise disciplines was one in which I challenged my cardiovascular system to the absolute limit for 26 continuous minutes every day. Sometimes I was not sure I could finish. To my surprise, even today, in my 80's, this rigorous workout is still increasing my endurance.

I firmly believe that I must exercise, not only to live one more day, but to live each day more fully.

DO I TRULY NEED PEOPLE IN MY LIFE?

> No man is an island,
> No man stands alone;
> Each man's joy is joy to me,
> Each man's grief is my own.
> We need one another,
> So I will defend
> Each man as my brother,
> Each man as my friend.
>
> John Donne

Up to this point, I had been very self-reliant; I never thought I needed the support of others. My success had depended completely on my own efforts of hard work and determination. However, the problems I experienced at the University of Iowa Medical School suggested that something was lacking. My strategy of being self-reliant had not helped me to reach my goal, even though I was highly skilled. What was missing?

Chapter 5

Before my father died, I am not sure whether I had ever thought about how much I truly needed other people in my life. In fact, I don't think that I really felt that I absolutely needed others.

At that time, I believed that if I were a good doctor, people would have confidence in me and I would have a busy practice without actively seeking patients. The question still remained … what kind of relationships would I have with people?

Could I imagine a situation that would help me determine if I needed people in my life? An image came into view. I pictured myself being alone on an uninhabited island. I asked myself if I could exist on that isolated island all by myself, armed only with the knowledge I had. I thought of all kinds of things that I would need.

What about water? Where would I find it? Would it be safe to drink? How would I determine that? Where would I find food? What would be safe to eat? How would I build a fire? What would I wear when my clothes wore out? What on earth would I do if I got sick? Who would take care of me?

The questions were endless. In the end, I had to admit I could not live on that island alone. I became convinced that to survive, I absolutely did need people for what they could do for me. I realized that it would be extremely difficult for me to live without the help of others.

Chapter 5

Do I Believe That I Could Enjoy Life Without People?

I had never thought of this question before. I asked myself whether I could live entirely alone. Wouldn't I be extremely lonely with no one to communicate with or confide in; no one to share feelings of happiness or sadness; no one to exchange knowledge with, to challenge or compete with? Most importantly, wouldn't I miss having friends?

I realized that my own happiness would largely depend upon the sort of relationships I had with others. It wasn't hard to convince myself that I truly needed people to enjoy life.

I needed people for what they could do for me and, more importantly, for what I could do for them.

Who Would Take Care of Me In Time of Financial Need?

My parents? Did they have the means to do it? Would it be fair to expect them to? Would they be around when I needed their support?

No, I could not count on my parents. My father was dead. My mother had enough assets to adequately take care of herself but not someone else. No, it would not be fair to depend on my mother. Also, she might not be around.

My brother? Wouldn't he have his own family to provide for?

No, I would not be able to rely on my brother in time of financial need. It just wouldn't be fair, and he might not be around when I needed him.

Chapter 5

Uncle Sam? Could I absolutely count on the government taking care of me?

No, that option was definitely out!

Other options? I came to the conclusion that there was only one person who could take care of me, and that person was *me and only me*.

This soul searching was extremely important to me. As I pondered these questions, my outlook on life was radically changed.

I was determined to immediately begin preparing for my future. I needed to become financially independent so I could take care of myself and my family. Later in my life, I could do what I wanted to do when I wanted to do it.

First Steps To A New Career

Chapter 6

How it Began: Dun and Bradstreet

After deciding not to continue on with my medical career, I searched for another challenging occupation that would be meaningful and exciting. A friend who lived next door had been a salesman with Dun and Bradstreet. He thought that I, too, possessed a good sales personality and offered to help me get started.

It is no use saying, "We are doing our best." You have got to succeed in doing what is necessary.

Winston Churchill

At that time, Dun and Bradstreet did not have any sales openings in the credit division within the Kansas City area. However, there was an opening in the collection division which sold services to companies that had difficulty collecting past due accounts. It sounded enticing. I was hired by Dun and Bradstreet, and the state of Kansas was assigned as my territory.

I called upon many businesses and convinced many to buy the collection service, which was not inexpensive. Other competitors offered the same service at a lower cost, but my company was considered the *Cadillac* of the industry.

As time went by, my clients informed me that Dun and Bradstreet was not delivering the quality of service that it had agreed to provide. This did not meet my own expectations. I had no choice but to seek another challenge in sales. Even so, I did make many new friends and learned a lot from this first experience in business.

Chapter 6

What I learned:

I truly enjoy selling.

People are open to ideas that can help them.

To be successful, it is important to earn the trust and confidence of others.

Whatever you offer must be absolutely the very best.

People do not object to high fees, but they do expect results.

People do not tolerate bad service or inferior products.

THE INVESTMENT BUSINESS

I began searching for another challenging opportunity in sales. Various life insurance companies wined and dined me to entice me to represent their companies. One successful agent even asked me to accompany him on several occasions to meet with his clients. After this experience, I decided that selling high-cost life insurance was just not for me.

When this particular agent finally realized that he was not going to be able to convince me to sell life insurance, he introduced me to the mutual fund concept. After hearing the details, I thought it was fantastic. People could pool their money with others and have their money managed continuously by professionals following a stated investment objective. I was excited. The agent handed me a large book on mutual funds and asked me to take it home and study it. He had an arrangement with a fund in St. Louis, called Associated Fund, that would pay me three percent of whatever I sold.

Chapter 6

After studying the book, I shared my enthusiasm about the mutual fund concept with my mother. She asked for information about the Associated Fund and suggested that before I made any decision, it might be wise to visit with someone else in the investment business and hear their point of view. A classmate of hers, Cameron Reed, was in the mutual fund business. In fact, he was the president of Waddell & Reed, a mutual fund underwriter.

When I went down to his office, Mr. Reed was not in. I was introduced to the office manager and told him about my plans to sell mutual funds. He suggested I consider representing the United Funds, a large mutual fund offered by Waddell & Reed. Instead of receiving a commission of only 3 percent from the much smaller Associated Fund, I would be able to receive 4 percent. Not surprisingly, I decided to join Waddell & Reed where I learned the mutual fund business from the ground up.

As a representative of Waddell & Reed, I was required to pay all my expenses – my income was based only on commissions. There would be absolutely no advances on future sales. My success depended on my salesmanship.

History of Mutual Funds

"It's difficult, perhaps impossible, to identify the exact moment when the mutual fund was born ... Yet, this much is certain: mutual funds sprang to life in the 1920's. By 1929 there were 19 "open-end" investment trusts. A new trust was being formed almost every day.

...Paul C. Cabot is one of the founding fathers of the mutual fund industry. In 1924 he was one of three money managers who founded the State Street Investment Trust, the nation's second oldest mutual fund."

from Max Rottersman and Jason Zweig
Friends of Financial History, Spring 1994

Chapter 6

MY MENTOR, GEORGE H. WOOD

During the late fall of 1953, I noticed a vice president of Waddell & Reed walking up the street by himself. He looked very impressive wearing a dark Homburg and a cashmere coat. I had not been introduced to him, but I thought, "Why not approach him and introduce myself?" Upon doing so, I learned his name was George H. Wood.

I mentioned that I was a new sales representative with the company and asked if he would help me learn the business.

George told me that he felt there were two ways to learn – study a few books written by experts or read the opinions of many people. When I assured him that I would prefer to learn a variety of views on a topic, he said he would suggest books for me to read but only if I agreed to study each one he selected. I was delighted.

George was a speed-reader who reviewed hundreds of books, but he shared with me only those he thought would be of

My mentor, George H. Wood.

value. I read a great many books that he had selected and underlined. That was the beginning of a fantastic relationship. We continued to have private sessions as long as he lived. My experience with George was worth more than my two college degrees. In fact, I like to think that I've earned a third degree from the School of Hard Knocks.

Chapter 6

DRESSING THE PART

George taught me that my appearance could affect the attitude that others had toward me.

One day, as I stood in front of his desk, he asked, "Would you rather have people concentrate on the tie you are wearing or on what you say?"

I answered, "On what I say."

Then he stated, "You had better find a more subdued tie to wear; one that does not attract so much attention."

At that time, sport clothes were my favorite attire. George mentioned that wearing sport clothes could possibly detract from what I said. "Why not dress to fit the image people expect? Why not look the part of a successful mutual funds representative?"

His suggestion made sense. I tried to improve my appearance by wearing conservative suits and ties, ones that would not be distracting. In the winter, I started to wear the same type of Homburg and cashmere overcoat that George wore because his appearance certainly impressed me. This style of dressing inspired me to live up to the image of a successful sales representative. Hopefully I impressed others in the same way that George impressed me.

THE IMPORTANCE OF A HANDSHAKE

I will never forget the time in 1954 when George greeted me with a handshake. I shook his hand, as I normally did. He hesitated, then asked, "What on earth were you trying to do?"

Chapter 6

I responded, "What do you mean?"

He answered, "What were you trying to accomplish when you shook my hand?"

"I was just shaking your hand."

"Aren't you aware that you had a fantastic opportunity to convey your sincere feelings towards me through your handshake?" he queried.

I was amazed. "I never thought of it that way."

He then asked me to shake hands with him again. My second handshake was probably not much better than the first, because I really did not know what to do.

George had me practice shaking hands with him many times. He had me come in and leave his office over and over again to shake his hand.

THE WRONG HANDSHAKE

When you shake hands, you are given the opportunity to convey your feelings of warmth and sincerity. I might miss this golden opportunity by using one of the following "wrong" handshakes:

Bone-crusher: Squeezing the other's hand too hard.

Dishrag: Letting your hand lie in the other person's hand with no energy in it.

Pump handle: Pumping the other's hand too vigorously.

Imprisoning: Holding the other's hand with both of your hands.

Chapter 6

THE RIGHT HANDSHAKE

I am aware that some people absolutely dislike being touched in any way, by anyone. They resent this familiarity and are naturally unfavorably impressed with your touch. However, a handshake is generally an accepted social practice when meeting people. George taught me how to make the best impression by developing a great handshake.

Reach out for the other person's hand and smile in a friendly way.

Hold the hand firmly and look sincerely into the person's eyes.

Greet him with your name or a warm, "Hello."

COMMUNICATE, DON'T INSTRUCT

At the time I was pouring over George's book selections, I was making my living entirely from commissions. I was learning the hard way that how you communicate with people means everything. George's handshaking lessons were one of the ways in which he hammered this home to me. He also told me, "You're not there to tell people what they **should** do. Your job is to make them aware of what they **can** do."

After I met with a prospective client, I would sit down and reconstruct our conversation in writing to make sure I had followed George's advice.

When I reflect on my five decades of business experience, it's clear that few people have had more influence on my life and the way I think than George. I am deeply indebted to him for everything he taught me. He made a tremendous difference in my life, and I will never forget what he did for me and my family.

Chapter 6

Don't Sell, Help People Succeed

Waddell & Reed expected me to convince people to make periodic monthly investments into one of their mutual funds. This new investment would be in addition to any other investments that person was making. After contacting hundreds of people, I realized that I had been trying to make sales for my own benefit; I wasn't thinking about what was best for my customers. It seemed as if I was carrying a great big sign on my back advertising Waddell & Reed. I felt as if I were a peddler, and I disliked this feeling. This was not what I truly wanted to do!

Finally, I determined that what I really wanted was to try to help people improve their financial positions rather than sell mutual funds for commissions. From that point on, I never tried to "sell mutual funds." My goal was to consider the whole person and what was best for him.

In order to be of help, I needed to understand what people wanted financially and how they planned to achieve their goals. Then I could use the knowledge that I possessed to help them improve their financial positions. This was a new idea – to act as a resource for people who needed more information in order to make good decisions about their financial futures.

Helping the Little Guy

In seeking to understand people's financial problems, I learned two important facts. First, I became aware that while many large investors were familiar with the mutual fund concept and had their own advisors, the small investors were not familiar with mutual funds and needed an advisor. Second, I discovered that many of the people I approached were life insurance poor.

Chapter 6

They were paying way too much for life insurance protection and, therefore, could not afford to invest. This bothered me.

Small investors were not familiar with mutual funds. Many people were life insurance poor.

It became clear that I needed to learn more about life insurance. I was introduced to a public life insurance actuary who spent many hours helping me understand the complexities of life insurance. I realized that people needed adequate life insurance protection before starting an investment plan.

To follow through with my vision of helping others improve their financial positions, I also became a life insurance agent offering the most life insurance protection for the least cost. In this way, my customers could buy more pure life insurance protection, cancel their old policies and invest their savings. They were able to be adequately protected by insurance **and have enough money leftover to invest in mutual funds**.

I am extremely proud that I had the wisdom to see that there is a tremendous difference between "helping people improve their financial positions" and "selling mutual funds for commissions." My reason for being in business is to help others be successful. This focus on others has led to my success.

However, my initiative to help people find extra money by switching to lower priced insurance was not appreciated by the insurance companies. They began to deny my clients' applications for new life insurance. It seemed I would need to start my own insurance company.

When the management of Waddell & Reed heard about my efforts, they were concerned about being associated with anyone having a life insurance company. They told me I could either forget about starting a life insurance company or leave.

I said, "Good-bye."

Chapter 6

A Cost Saving Example

In 1955, a prominent plastic surgeon was paying $7,000 a year for $100,000 of high cost life insurance protection. I provided the same amount of annual renewable term life insurance to him, renewable to age 100, for only $700 a year. He invested the difference of $6,300 a year in mutual funds. I helped him improve his financial position.

The present value of that $7,000 insurance premium, 50 years later, adjusted for the loss in value of a dollar, was about $50,000.

STOWERS & COMPANY

Since I wanted to remain in the mutual fund business, I needed to form a broker/dealer company that could offer mutual funds. Stowers & Company was incorporated in Missouri on May 16, 1956, as a broker/dealer and was registered with the Securities & Exchange Commission in Washington, D.C.

I bought the initial ten shares of the common stock of the company for $500 at $50 a share. The company almost immediately needed more money for its operation, so two months later I bought 20 more shares of common stock, also at $50 a share. My personal investment amounted to just $1,500.

The company headquarters was in my small one-bedroom apartment on the second floor of a building at 312 West 46 Terrace, in Kansas City, Missouri.

We initially had only two officers: My uncle, Richard King Smith, was President, and I was Vice President and Treasurer. Later, Amos A. Hermanson, Jr., a CPA in private practice, became director and secretary of Stowers & Company. He was responsible for maintaining the financial records of the company and eventually became my partner.

Chapter 6

Amos introduced me to his friend, Francis J. Raw, a member of his church. Frank was much older than the rest of us and became our "father" and mentor until he died in 1987. We were extremely fortunate to have Frank with us. He was wise and had experience with several businesses before joining our little company. We are indebted to Frank's ability to foresee the consequences of making the wrong decision.

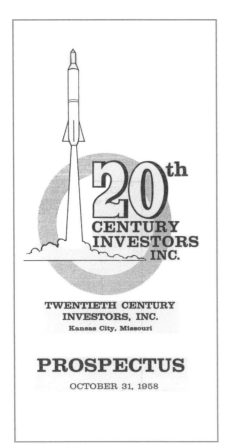

Cover of Prospectus, October 31, 1958.

Mr. Stowers would come and pick Mr. Raw up for lunch pretty much every day. Over lunch, they would discuss whatever the hot topic was for the day. They didn't always agree, and their discussions could get hot. However, they were always very respectful of each other. You could tell they really enjoyed each other's company.

After lunch, Mr. Raw would sometimes take a nap on the couch in Mr. Stowers' office. If Jim had a meeting while Mr. Raw was napping, he'd use the lobby. I thought that was so considerate.

Martha Miller, an early employee

To begin with, our company sold all the big named funds with only a handful of sales representatives. They were happy to work with us because we offered a high commission.

Chapter 6

SURVIVORS' BENEFIT INSURANCE COMPANY

As I was setting up Stowers & Company, I continued to research what I needed to do to begin offering my mutual fund customers the most life insurance protection for the least amount of money. I had become convinced that low-cost, permanent, annual renewable term policies represented the best value.

Since in the 50's few life insurance companies were willing to offer this kind of policy, my public actuary suggested that I consider starting my own life insurance company. He informed me that it was possible to start a Stipulated Premium Life Insurance company in the State of Missouri for only $50,000.

A group of us decided to form a life insurance company that would sell the kind of policy we would be willing to buy ourselves. Among us, we raised the $50,000 needed to start the new company.

What should we call it? We wanted a name that would best describe the type of insurance we planned to offer. Someone suggested we call it "Death Benefit Insurance Company." This was, perhaps, too accurate a name. Our medical director suggested that we breathe some life into it by calling it "Survivors' Benefit Insurance Company." Of course, we agreed.

Chapter 6

Because we started our company with limited capital, we absolutely had to show a profit each year in order to remain in business. Furthermore, before we could offer life insurance to the public, we were required by the State of Missouri to:

Convince 100 people to acquire life insurance policies;
Collect the full first annual premium;
Deliver the policies;
Inform the insured that the policies would not be in effect
until all 100 policies were delivered.

Accomplishing that was quite a challenge, but we overcame it and began to help our new investors. We were proud of our little life insurance company that was authorized to be a stipulated Premium Life Insurance company in Missouri in 1957. As far as we knew, it was the first company to offer **pure permanent annual renewable term insurance** renewable to age 100.

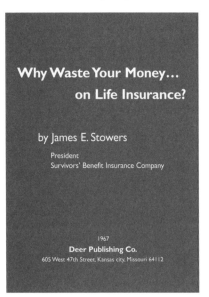

Our concept regarding life insurance was extremely important. Communicating that information to others was time consuming. I determined that I could reach many more people by putting down all the facts in writing. So I wrote a book, *Why Waste Your Money on Life Insurance?*

As time went on, Survivors' Benefit Insurance Company was admitted to do business in 23 states. It eventually got to the point where we needed to invest more capital, time and energy in order for the business to continue to grow.

Chapter 6

Our group of investors owned a little more than 30 percent of the company and was not interested in adding any additional capital to improve the value of the remaining 70 percent. More importantly, we did not have the extra time or energy. We needed to concentrate on the fund business.

In 1980, we sold Survivors' Benefit Insurance Company to Penn Mutual. The original investors of the insurance company earned eight times their initial investment … not a bad result.

Here I am in 1964, wearing a Homburg and cashmere coat,
on the way to church with my young family.

117

Chapter 7

Setting Up Our
Own Mutual Funds

**"J. E. Stowers Maps
A World Wide Plan
of Investment Selling"**

KC Star – October 31, 1958

Chapter 7

SETTING UP OUR OWN MUTUAL FUNDS

After reviewing the financial results of Stowers & Company at the end of 1957, we determined that the company was not earning enough money for all its efforts. We had to either find a strategy for becoming more profitable in the investment business or look for opportunities elsewhere. Since we liked the business we were in, we needed to search for a way to increase our income.

Pick out something you enjoy doing that you are passionate about, then do it. It will not end up being only an 8-hour a day job.

Winston Churchill

One possibility was to create our own mutual fund complex so we could retain the entire sales charge. We could have a gross profit of 2.5 percent while still paying 5.4 percent sales commission out of an 8.5 percent sales charge. That decision would create a gross profit of four times the previous 0.6 percent.

We didn't want to offer just another average mutual fund. It had to be the very best, or we didn't want to be part of it. Our mutual fund would have to be recognized for:

> *Having the best investment objective.*
>
> *Offering the best investment programs.*
>
> *Having the best investment management.*
>
> *Having the best custodian bank.*
>
> *Employing the best accounting firm.*
>
> *Having the best service operation.*

Chapter 7

In addition, we realized we would have to:

Have the best legal help.

Use temporary capital from additional investors.

Hire the best investment team.

Develop the best investment plan.

We asked ourselves, "Is our dream of creating a new mutual fund overly ambitious?" Did others believe that Amos, Frank and I had the business experience, education, ability and determination to provide people with the best mutual fund – one having the best future investment record and best service? Could we convince others we would likely be successful?

An even bigger question was, could we convince others to believe in our dream so strongly that they would be anxious to share in our future success by owning a part of our company and helping initially to finance it?

To find out what others thought, I proceeded to ask successful business people, bankers and other professionals for their opinions. I asked them if they thought I was too young to accomplish this and if they thought the idea was overly ambitious. After they had heard the whole story, no one attempted to discourage our effort. We decided to proceed to create our mutual fund organization.

"I started at a time when we dreamed of millions, not billions. All 15 of us crowded into the basement office of a bank in Kansas City's Country Club Plaza with no computers, no imaging and no indication of what Twentieth Century would become."

Dennis von Waaden
From the *Centurion*, December, 1998

121

Chapter 7

Finding the Best Legal Help

One of the most important pieces of business advice I ever received came from my mother, who insisted that I have the very best qualified attorney. She suggested that we consult with an attorney friend she had known for years who had an outstanding reputation, Alfred Kuraner.

We met with Alfred and informed him of our plans. He was impressed but indicated his practice was too large to accept a new client. However, he suggested we consider his brother, a lawyer who had just returned to Kansas City after practicing in New York City.

Irving Kuraner

We were so impressed with Irving Kuraner that we immediately asked him to do our legal work. He was fabulous. We later learned that he was a Phi Beta Kappa graduate of the Columbia Law School.

He was a fantastic attorney and became a very close friend. We are extremely indebted to him for helping us become so successful and enabling us to remain in business. In my opinion, the company would not be in this business today if it were not for him.

We needed to define our corporate structure. I remembered how Waddell & Reed was organized into three different companies: the fund was called United Funds, Inc.; the investment manager was Continental Research Corporation; and the company that sold the fund shares was Waddell & Reed, Inc.

I had no idea why the management of those companies had decided on that corporate structure, but I was convinced that they must have had a very good reason for doing so. Since their organization was successful and

Chapter 7

it appeared logical to me, I decided to use that same corporate structure. In our case, the fund would be called Twentieth Century Investors Inc.; the investment manager would be Investors Research Corporation; and the underwriter would be Stowers & Company.

STOWERS & COMPANY STRUCTURE

Having the underwriter separate from the investment manager proved to be very effective. Initially, this made us appear bigger than we were. This organizational structure separated individual functions. For example, one company was for sales and financial service, while the other company was the investment manager. This allowed us to separate the regulatory authorities. If the two companies were combined, the entire operation would be regulated by the National Association of Securities Dealers; the various state securities departments; and the federal Securities and Exchange Commission.

From the October 31, 1958 Prospectus.

With the two companies separate, only the sales and financial service company (Stowers & Company) was subject to all the regulations. Investment Research Corporation was subject only to the federal Securities and Exchange Commission regulation and the securities department of the State of Missouri.

This structure caused a great deal of curiosity and confusion to anyone who was trying to determine the financial results of our entire operation without having the financial statements of both companies available to them at the same time.

Chapter 7

As for the financial structure of the companies in the organization, the sales company, Stowers & Company, would probably need the most assets. We decided that 80 percent of the capital should be invested in Stowers & Company and the remaining 20 percent invested in Investors Research Corporation. The fund, Twentieth Century Investors, Inc., would be entirely owned by fund shareholders.

Twentieth Century Investors, Inc.
4725 Wyandotte
Kansas City, Missouri

INVESTMENT MANAGER
Investors Research Corporation
Kansas City, Missouri

UNDERWRITER
Stowers & Company
Kansas City, Missouri

LEGAL COUNSEL
Kuraner, Freeman, Kuraner & Oberlander
Kansas City, Missouri

CUSTODIAN
United States Trust Company of New York
New York, New York

REGISTRAR
United States Trust Company of New York
New York, New York

AUDITORS
Arthur Andersen & Co.
Kansas City, Missouri

From the October 31, 1958 Prospectus.

Chapter 7

To simplify matters, I am going to discuss the structure as though it was only one company, although in actuality, both companies were organized the same way.

It was determined that we would need about $100,000 of temporary capital to make the companies financially secure over time. This would cover organizational expenses and some shared general office expenses with the life insurance company.

We did not write a "business plan" to determine the amount of money we needed. I had no idea I was supposed to do such a plan and, furthermore, I did not know what a business plan was since my education was in medicine. We did, however, try to determine exactly how much money was needed. We then doubled that amount to arrive at $100,000. We were determined to stay within that budget.

START-UP FINANCING

After Irving Kuraner completed the legal work to form the company, we turned to the question of how to obtain our start-up financing. The concept that Irving came up with was absolutely critical to our success. He cautioned that if we offered investors only common stock in order to obtain our initial financing, we would greatly dilute our own interest in the company. Think of it as a pie. If you serve someone half a pie, you have only one-half remaining for yourself. However, if you serve only a quarter of the pie, you have three quarters remaining.

To achieve this kind of distribution, Irving suggested we consider using primarily **non**-cumulative preferred stock, along with a small amount of common stock, to obtain the initial operating capital.

Chapter 7

The idea intrigued us. Irving asked how much of the common stock we each wanted to own. I wanted one-half of the common stock and my partner, Amos A. Hermanson, Jr., a CPA, asked for one-fourth of the common stock. Irving then suggested that we authorize 4,000 shares of common stock having a par value of $1.00 and 1,000 shares of 5 percent **non**-cumulative preferred stock having a par value of $100. The preferred stock would not pay any cash dividend, but its value would increase each year by 5 percent until the company repurchased the stock. **The remaining 25 percent of the common stock was used as an incentive for people to become investors.**

OPERATING CAPITAL

We reorganized Stowers & Company. I returned the stock I had originally purchased and bought 2,000 shares of common stock for $2,000. (This is the amount that became worth more than $1 billion 40 years later.) My partner, Amos, bought 1,000 shares of common stock for $1,000. Neither he nor I bought any of the **non**-cumulative preferred stock. We would offer each of the other interested investors 50 shares of common stock for $50 and 50 shares of the 5 percent **non**-cumulative preferred stock for $5,000. These outside investors were unable to buy the **common stock**, with its potential for great rewards, unless they bought the **non**-*cumulative preferred stock*. It was the preferred

Cumulative Preferred Stock promises to pay its dividend no matter what, even if it can't be paid on time.

People who own ***Common Stock*** *in a company have voting rights in the company. They may receive dividends if the board of directors declares dividends. The value of the stock goes up as the earnings and revenues of the company increase.*

Chapter 7

stock that gave us our operating capital. It is important to note that everyone bought the common stock at the same $1.00 par value.

To find our outside investors, I turned to people in a field that I knew well – medical doctors.

The first doctor I tried to interest in investing told me we had the investment plan backwards. He said my partner and I should limit ourselves to 25 percent of the common stock and let the outside investors, those putting up the most money, take 75 percent. "No way," I said. "We are taking the 75 percent because we are investing our time to make the company a success. After all, what is going to make the new management company successful in the future? Is it the power of all the money it invests, or is it the absolute determination, dedication and time devoted by management to make the company successful?" **Time, energy and determination create money.**

Another doctor who witnessed this exchange became our first outside investor. Nine other people, six of them medical doctors, also invested. Each bought 50 shares of common stock for $50 and 50 shares of 5 percent non-cumulative preferred stock for $5,000. Other transactions later brought in additional capital.

A lot of venture capitalists would agree with the doctor who thought my partner and I should take only a minority stake. However, investors must understand that when they are about to invest in something they expect to be successful, they must be assured that those people actually doing the work have the incentive to do their best.

You must convince people of your dream, and then convince them you have the ability to make your dream become a reality.

There are two advantages for investors who put most of their money in preferred stock. First, when the preferred stock is repurchased in the future, the investor receives the increased repurchase amount and then retains only

Chapter 7

the common stock. Second, if the business does not succeed, there is a greater chance that they will get some, or most, of the money back because preferred stockholders are paid first.

To the best of our ability, we had calculated our start-up costs. We were determined that we would not use more money than we had originally planned. We were convinced that the future success of the company would rest entirely upon management's absolute determination to succeed through its commitment of time and energy.

When one dreams alone, it is only a dream.
When we dream together, it is the beginning of reality.

SEARCHING FOR THE RIGHT CUSTODIAN BANK

We realized that people tend to judge you by the company you keep, so the image of the bank we would use as a custodian bank would be extremely important. It would have to be well-known and enjoy an outstanding reputation. One bank had been suggested to us that might meet our criteria, Bankers Trust.

Frank Raw, Amos Hermanson and I decided to go to New York to meet the head of the custodian bank, as well as various investment firms, in order to learn what they might have to offer us. We wanted to observe their operations and determine whether we wanted to do business with them.

Chapter 7

More importantly, as we were trying to locate the very best investment management, we wanted to learn where the bank believed they were receiving the best equity investment advice for their trust department.

Bankers Trust's offices were very impressive. The ceilings seemed to be 100 feet high. We were in awe of the large pillars holding up the ceiling. The trust officer was informed about who we were and what we were trying to do. We said we were interested in learning about his bank and the services it offered. Time was short, so we mentioned that our main interest was learning what he personally thought was his bank's best source of equity investment information.

He reviewed with us the names of several investment firms that he believed provided the bank with the best research and recommendations within various sectors of the market. We noted that the names of several investment firms appeared repeatedly under different sectors - Smith Barney being one of them. We noted those investment firms. We asked the trust officer if he would mind if we met later in the day with his associates in the custody department. It was agreed that we would come back and meet with them during lunch.

During the rest of the morning, we visited with at least four different investment firms and listened to their stories. Each firm was asked to explain its philosophy and why it was the best. We made every effort to be impartial.

Chapter 7

MEETING RALPH JOHNSON

I still remember the details of the meeting we had at Smith Barney when we were introduced to Ralph B. Johnson, the head of the Planned Investment Department. We asked Ralph to explain his investment philosophy and review with us his investment results. We were impressed with Ralph right away, but we tried to keep an open mind.

Ralph asked if we had chosen a custodian bank. We indicated that we had not yet made that decision, but we were seriously considering Bankers Trust. Ralph suggested we also consider the United States Trust Company of New York, the largest trust company in the world. He gave us permission to mention his name if we decided to see them. We thanked him for his suggestion and left for lunch with Bankers Trust.

At lunch, the officers of the custody department indicated they wanted to work with us. They showed us all the individual forms they wanted us to use and how much their custodian fees would amount to.

Taking Ralph Johnson's advice, we also visited the United States Trust Company which said that they, too, would like to work with us. When we asked what they expected of us, (what forms they wanted us to use) their answer amazed us. They said, "What do you want us to do?" They had no special forms. When they informed us what their custodian fee would be, we were shocked. We estimated that their fee was about one-tenth of what Bankers Trust Company wanted to charge us.

We tried to remain open minded when we returned to Kansas City to present our new stockholders with our findings. All three of us who went to New York recommended that we work with Ralph B. Johnson of Smith

Chapter 7

Barney and select the largest trust company in the world, United States Trust Company of New York, to be our custodian bank. The stockholders asked if Ralph could come back to Kansas City for a short meeting and presentation.

After Ralph's presentation in Kansas City, everyone agreed with our choice. He became a member of the investment committee of Investors Research. This was the beginning of a fantastic association. We will always be indebted to him for what he did. I consider Ralph my investment father.

THE VALUE OF ATTRACTING THE VERY BEST PEOPLE

From the beginning, I was aware that I needed to surround myself with the very best people. It would have been an accident if we had become successful without them. Since I did not know all the answers, we needed to attract and retain the people who were experts in their fields.

With the choice of Arthur Anderson as our accounting firm, we finally realized that we had the team we needed to offer our clients the best mutual fund products. We felt our fund would not only be different but would stand out when compared with other funds. Our fund would be unique.

The decisions we made that first year laid the foundations of the company. It started with my dream to

I studied the lives of great men and famous women, and I found that the men and women who got to the top were those who did the jobs they had in hand, with everything they had of energy and enthusiasm and hard work.

Harry S. Truman

131

Chapter 7

help other people be successful. The next most important step was to follow my mother's advice to only associate with and hire the most qualified people and the best services. I did this by associating with:

Irving Kuraner, lawyer

Frank Raw, business mentor

Ralph Johnson, investment adviser

United States Trust Company of New York, custodian bank

I have continued to follow this advice and can summarize my experience:

Everything, and I emphasize everything, is possible if you associate with the very best people.

Search for and attract the best people – then do your utmost to retain them.

Encourage them to become your friend – rather than hiring friends, overlooking their abilities and qualifications.

The best people help make the best company.

CREATING OUR FIRST FUNDS

In the late 50's, there were only 250 mutual funds (compared to the 10,000 offered today) and only a small percentage of households had even heard of a mutual fund. We decided to focus on the small investors who truly needed our help. They did not have available to them the services we offered and would more likely be open to new ideas. We would offer them a choice of two excellent mutual funds and Pure Annual Renewable Term Life Insurance so they that could afford to invest.

Chapter 7

We had already determined that we would offer a growth fund and an income fund. Twentieth Century Growth Investors was the fund we created for people who wanted their money to grow. For people who were interested in receiving income, we created an excellent income fund, Twentieth Century Income Investors.

"We wanted to be the best fund in the country – a fund that we would be willing to buy ourselves."

Our challenge was to convince people to invest their hard earned money in a brand new mutual fund – one that had no investment record and no sound record of integrity. We were confident that the best mutual fund with no investment record, would be more appealing than a mutual fund having only an average ten-year record. With very talented and dedicated fund representatives, we had no doubt that we could convince people that we had a unique, high quality product.

PERIODIC PAYMENT PLAN

To help our fund representatives get started, we gave them the most generous commission in the business – 5.4 percent. We then devised a unique payment plan that would enable investors to accumulate shares of the growth fund, while giving our sales representatives the financial incentive they needed.

Our investment plan offered a 10-year periodic payment plan so investors could accumulate Growth Investors shares. Plans were offered in amounts to suit every budget: $25, $50, $75, $100 and $200 monthly plans were available. We were absolutely convinced that these products were of superb quality.

Chapter 7

Over half of the sales charge for the entire plan was deducted out of the first year payments. The plan was unique because it had a "Completion Rebate" paid at the time of completion. Sales representatives were compensated entirely out of the first year's payments.

THE SECURITIES AND EXCHANGE COMMISSION BALKS

We had preliminary discussions with the SEC regarding our plans. They informed us that they had no problem with our establishing the two different types of funds. However, they said the investors in our plan would have to write their monthly payments to United States Trust Company rather than to the Periodic Payment Plan in which they were investing.

I spent a lot of time in the research library of the SEC in Washington, D.C. trying to understand why our investors had to write their checks to our custodian bank. We believed that investors were investing their money in our Periodic Payment Plan, not in the custodian bank. Our main competition was doing exactly what we wanted to do. Why did the SEC make an exception for us?

We decided to change the name of the plan to Twentieth Century Investors Plan. I then went directly to the SEC's Legal Counsel in Washington, D.C. and got permission for investors to write their monthly checks to Twentieth Century Investors Plan.

With the SEC finally off our backs, the periodic payment plans were able to fuel our early beginnings. They enabled us to pay the sales representatives, created income that helped us to remain in business and

Chapter 7

enabled our investors to accumulate shares in a great mutual fund at a rate they could afford.

However, in 1970 the SEC changed the law regarding periodic payment plans. The new law required an investor be given the right to change his mind anytime within 12 months after purchasing a plan and ask for the return of all his money. This created a huge liability for our company, since up to one-half of the first year's investment would have already been paid out to sales representatives. The liability would be further increased by any loss in value of the amount actually invested in mutual fund shares. Because of this potential liability, we were forced to discontinue offering these plans in 1971. If the purpose of the new law was to discourage funds from offering such plans, it achieved its purpose.

By this time, we did not need the financial continuity provided by periodic payment plans. Nevertheless, we were extremely fortunate to have had this plan while it lasted. It would have been extremely difficult to build the company without it, because the program allowed the sales representatives to earn enough money to remain in the business. It was our cornerstone.

With our management team in place; talented, dedicated sales representatives; and the confidence that we had the best funds; we were ready for business.

"I've represented a number of successful businessmen in my time. They're all quite different except for one thing; they are just always persistent as hell. They just won't give up. That was Jim. He would not give up. He was too sure the time would come when he'd be successful."

Irving Kuraner, Chief Legal Counsel, for Twentieth Century, 1956.

Helping People Improve Their Financial Positions

Here's what I believe:

*If you don't think that tomorrow is
going to be better than today, why get
up? You've got to believe each new
day is going to be better, and you
have to be determined to make it so.
If you are determined, then certainly,*
the best is yet to be.

The Eternal Bull

BY JACK JONATHAN

The character of a man emerges when he overcomes challenges, disappointments and accepts ever increasing responsibilities.

Jim's character was constantly tested because he held onto his belief that he could succeed in business by helping others rather than focusing only on the bottom line.

In these chapters, you will discover that Jim had an insatiable curiosity and a knack for innovation. From his early beginnings, he realized that he could not do everything himself. Instead, he selected people who shared his values and were the very best in areas in which he had no training or expertise. The company thrived because of Jim's sincere belief in teamwork and the way he inspired and challenged the very best people.

Chapter 8

Innovating in Mutual Funds

Chapter 8

INNOVATING IN MUTUAL FUNDS

Twentieth Century Investors

If you help people become financially successful, in time they will help you become successful.

Although we were incorporated in Delaware as Twentieth Century Investors in December of 1957, it took some time to get through the details of setting up the business. Finally, on October 31, 1958, we were ready to offer two mutual fund classes to the public: Twentieth Century Growth Investors and Twentieth Century Income Investors. We had a nice office in the basement of the Country Club Bank at 4724 Wyandotte Street, Kansas City, Missouri.

In November 1958, to attract more people to invest in the fund, we put ads in the paper saying that the funds would be free of a sales charge until December 31st. After that, the charge would be 8.5 percent.

I will always remember that last day of 1958. It was snowing hard. Our office was small. New investors were standing in line outside in the snow, waiting to invest at the last minute. We had everybody completing applications until well into the evening. The total assets in the funds at the end of 1958 were $405,164.

Fund Management

Money management of the funds was extremely important. Ralph Johnson of Smith Barney, our investment expert, was on our investment committee and made the decisions as to which stocks to buy and sell. Early on, it came to our attention that this arrangement might be improper. It was

Chapter 8

suggested that we hire our own portfolio manager. The final investment decisions would be his, but he could always listen to Ralph's advice. Ralph suggested a young man, Paul Pilling, who had worked with him for several years. We were impressed with Paul and invited him to join our team as our portfolio manager.

Paul worked in New York City in a one-room office with no windows, one floor below Smith Barney's office in the New York Stock Exchange Building. Paul made all the buy and sell decisions for the funds. However, he did not have far to go to consult with Ralph Johnson.

Ralph remained on our advisory committee and attended meetings regularly in Kansas City. He was a fantastic person. We were fortunate in having this extraordinary, self-made multi-millionaire help us in every way he could.

The Threat

Up to January 1968, our mutual funds had an excellent investment record. Then investigators from the SEC interrogated Paul Pilling about the funds' portfolio turnover.

Following the interrogation, Paul froze at the controls. He was afraid to make many investment decisions because he was convinced that he would be second-guessed by the SEC.

He was unquestionably frightened. I asked him why he was so afraid. He indicated that just before the SEC questioned him, they informed him that if he was found to have turned over the portfolios of the funds excessively, he could be fined $10,000, sent to prison and barred from the investment business for life. Paul took this threat to heart.

Chapter 8

I assured him that he had done a fantastic job of managing the funds. He had done nothing improper. He had done only what he was convinced was the correct way to manage the funds.

The SEC did not proceed further with their interrogation. Nevertheless, Paul remained afraid to make timely investment decisions and the performance of the funds went down. We lost Paul Pilling at the end of 1970 because he could not take the pressure of the SEC investigation.

The Stowers System: *Money Follows Earnings*

I took over management of the fund portfolios. Paul had given me quite a list of brokers that he had relied upon to select securities. He ranked them in order of importance. He also cautioned me not to listen to "curbstone" opinions.

Paul's brokers started calling with investment suggestions. I would write down the information they gave me and then study it. I would ask myself, "Why is this particular security so wonderful?" I remembered Ralph Johnson saying, *money follows earnings.* I respected Ralph's belief, but how could it be measured?

It took a lot of work to analyze these recommendations and make the correct decisions. Out of ten suggestions that I received from the brokers, I would

The Stowers System

The key to investing is that money follows earnings. To determine where the money is, we analyze companies and choose those whose earnings and revenues are accelerating. In this system, stocks inside a fund are bought and sold according to the financial results.

Chapter 8

select maybe only one stock to buy. This ratio was about the same with all of the brokers. However, I ended up selecting seven out of ten of the security recommendations that were given to me by Dick Dreihaus of Chicago. His recommendations proved more reliable and, therefore, less work for me.

It's not guesswork. I don't play that game. I won't even put 25 cents in a slot machine because the odds are against you. I want the odds on my side.

I called and asked him what on earth he was doing. When I learned that he was searching for companies that had accelerated earnings and revenues, I suddenly realized that this was a unique analytical method of measuring how *money follows earnings*. Naturally, I started working more closely with Dick and adopted his method of identifying successful companies.

In order to follow his approach, I needed four or five years of quarterly history on a company. I was performing all my calculations by hand and the information was not readily available in one place. It was very time consuming, and I was able to do only 35 calculations a day using a Hewlett Packard hand calculator.

I enjoyed the work but wanted to create the number one fund in the country, not the number two. Even though I was working seven days a week, we were not analyzing all the securities that were reporting earnings. We were cherry picking, that is picking and choosing certain stocks that we thought were good. I told Dick, "If I'm going to stay in this business, I've got to do something differently. If we want to be number one, we must analyze *all* the securities that report earnings and identify those whose earnings and revenues are accelerating." We needed a computer to find all the answers.

Chapter 8

DETERMINED TO MEET THE CHALLENGE

In 1971, when I asked IBM if they could program a computer that could analyze companies the way I did, they said "Yes." I agreed to lease a computer from them if they could program it using my approach.

The IBM programmer who had been assigned to help realized after a week that I knew what I wanted to do. She said, "Jim, since you know what you want, we will teach you how to program COBOL. Then we will write the program that will allow the computer terminal to communicate with the main-frame computer."

I burned the midnight oil teaching myself to program using three program instruction manuals. Then I designed and wrote a very detailed flow chart for the logic of the whole program. Because there would be tens of thousands of lines of code, and the system at the time had only 64K of memory, we had to shoehorn programs into memory by using multiple overlays.

By the time our mainframe computer was delivered in 1973, I had completed writing the program. Initially, we entered financial data of 2,300 individual companies.

The Creative Mind Never Sleeps

Learning to program the computer was almost a full time job in itself. I worked on it constantly.

One time, Virginia and I were at a conference in Montreal, and it suddenly came to me how to solve a certain programming problem. It was in the middle of the night and I did not want to wake Virginia up.

Where could I go? I finally went into the bathroom, shut the door and sat in the bathtub programming the darn thing.

Chapter 8

The financial data on the remaining companies was entered manually from a computer terminal.

The most dangerous thing that someone could do is to invest in a company that isn't accelerating.

After entering the fundamentals into the computer, we immediately knew if the earnings and revenues of that stock were truly accelerating. I wanted to be ahead of the curve, rather than trying to catch the rise when it was almost over. We took advantage of the inefficiency in market research. We would buy the stock before it became general knowledge that the company was accelerating and poised to go straight through the roof.

The Stowers System was extremely efficient in helping us identify successful companies in which to invest. The investment record of the two funds reflected that success.

AHEAD OF THE CURVE

I received a call from a brokerage firm in California which did really good work.

The broker wanted to recommend five great stocks to me. I said, "Fred, I don't know how to tell you this, but I already own four of those stocks, and I don't want to buy the fifth one."

He was flabbergasted. "I just came from the research department. How long have you owned them?"

I said, "I have owned them for about two months."

At first, I programmed only the earnings. Then Dick Dreihaus suggested I do the same thing for revenues. So we then had both earnings and revenues.

Chapter 8

The Stowers System became the cornerstone of our funds, allowing us to pick the best stocks ahead of other mutual fund companies. It also became a useful tool to convince portfolio managers around the country of the excellent performance of our funds.

I was looking for a way to demonstrate the system to more people, when I saw an advertisement for GMC's amazing new motor home. I was extremely impressed and convinced that the motor home would be an innovative and practical solution for meeting with prospective portfolio managers. Moreover, it would give our family a great way to see the country on vacations.

Although I was convinced that the motor home was really needed, it took me a little longer to convince Virginia. Finally, in 1974 Virginia and I went to the factory to take possession of our shiny, yellow motor home. Thus began our family trips to Florida and California.*

*See appendix III, Enjoying the Very Best

Virginia and me beside the yellow motor home.

Chapter 8

DROPPING THE SALES CHARGE

The performance of the funds was outstanding. We developed our own sales organization in Missouri, Kansas and Minnesota, with about 100 people representing our company.

Like most mutual funds offered at the time, investors had to pay a sales charge up front which was shared by the broker, the salesman and the fund. We had many conversations with various investment brokers about offering our funds.

Even though our funds' commissions were extremely high when compared to other funds, the brokers wanted additional incentives. When we said no to these "give ups," the brokers showed no interest in offering their customers the opportunity to buy our outstanding, successful funds.

Because of the long, depressing decline of the stock market in the early 1970's, most of our sales representatives moved on to greener pastures. Apparently no one wanted to work for their part of the sales charge. Because of the sales charge, we determined that we were making it hard for interested investors to buy our funds. We were making very few sales, so we did not see how things could be much worse without a sales charge.

On December 6, 1974, we dropped it and became no-load funds. Investments into the funds did not increase much. However, we felt we had made a wise decision because we had eliminated a huge barrier for potential investors – the high sales charge.

There are thousands of smaller investors for each large investor. I liked the no-load idea because it appealed to small investors who did not have a broker. This was in keeping with my belief that if we helped make people successful, they would, in turn, help make us successful.

Chapter 8

GIFTRUST™

At the birth of each of his grandchildren, Frank Raw made it a tradition to give each child a $1,000 investment in Twentieth Century Growth Investors. He had the investment registered in the name of the parent who was a custodian under the Uniform Gifts to Minors Act. When the grandchild came of age, the investment was transferred directly to the grandchild.

Frank became frustrated because he was unable to convince his grandchildren to leave his gift in the fund and give it a chance to really grow in value over time. I suggested he talk to our attorney to see if there was a legal way that an investment gift could be locked in for as long as he wanted so that it would have a real opportunity to grow in value.

The problem with this idea is that a young person might have a real need for that gift before it is available. But Frank and I agreed that each person has an obligation to provide for his own needs in life. Also, the recipient of such a gift could witness first hand what happens when investments are left undisturbed over time.

Our attorney, Irving Kuraner, designed the fund and called it Giftrust. It is a unique and irrevocable declaration of trust that cannot be changed in any way once it has been established. To help the creator of a Giftrust be remembered by the beneficiary, the registration of the account is set up to include a two-line message from the creator. Each year until the maturity of the Giftrust, the beneficiary receives mailings with a message from the creator of the trust.

On a personal level, the Giftrust concept truly has a heart. It generates an emotional response that connects the creator and the beneficiary throughout the life of the gift.

Chapter 8

On January 5, 1970, my mother was the first to establish a Giftrust – one for each of her seven grandchildren. Her initial gift was $250, which by 2005 had grown to $17,454. The grandchildren have been able to watch her gift grow, but they will not be able to touch it until the anniversary of their grandmother's birthday on November 14, 2015.

CHECK-A-MONTH™

When we first created Twentieth Century Investors in 1958, one of the funds paid quarterly dividends. The amount paid out each quarter varied according to the dividends the fund received from the portfolio investments during that quarter. These amounts were unpredictable and erratic. Moreover, any profits realized by the fund on portfolio sales during the year could only be paid in the final quarter of the year.

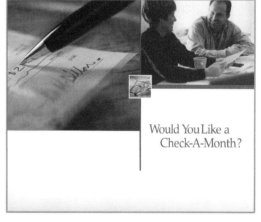

Would You Like a Check-A-Month?

Fund investors complained bitterly because they wanted to know ahead of time what amount they would receive and when they would receive it. Under the circumstances, it was impossible to meet their requests.

We began to realize that many investors were dependent on their dividend checks as though they were paychecks. One possible solution to this problem was a simple, convenient and automatic plan that assured investors they would receive a predetermined amount of money on a particular day of each month.

Chapter 8

To meet this need, we created Check-a-Month.™ We discontinued distributing dividends quarterly and paid them yearly instead. We reinvested any additional investment income and capital gain distributions. Then we offered our investors a fixed check each month, while continuing to professionally manage the balance of the investors' shares. Since 1971, the long-term results of the Check-a-Month plan in Growth Investors have been absolutely amazing, especially when you realize that they cover a period of time when the dollar lost over 80 percent of its value.

MONEY MAGAZINE

Early in 1981, a reporter with *Money* magazine called to request an interview for an article she was writing about the investment results of Growth Investors. Over the five years ending December 31, 1980, the fund had appreciated 467 percent or an average annual rate of 41 percent, making it the top fund in the country. She indicated that the magazine was also interviewing six other portfolio managers.

I agreed to be interviewed – provided that I would not be asked any questions about the names of stocks presently held in the portfolio or favored by me currently. Our directors believed this information to be private to our fund.

The reporter agreed with my conditions and I was interviewed. I was photographed jogging in the park early one morning. Later the reporter called to say she had some good news and some bad news. The good news was that *Money* magazine wanted to place my picture on the cover of the magazine. The bad news was that they wanted a more formal photograph.

Chapter 8

Jim jogging in the park.

Chapter 8

I was not surprised when the reporter told me I was the only one out of the seven people being featured in the issue who would not talk about the names of his portfolio holdings.

With the flattering picture of me on the front cover of *Money* magazine, and with our good track record, the phones started ringing off the hook. Overnight people realized that the Stowers System helped produce an outstanding investment record. The work began to pile up and it got really hectic.

I won't forget Jim and Virginia down there on the floor with all the staff, answering phones and filling in forms.

They called in for pizza. We were just one, big family getting the job done.

Debbie McMullin, employee

I called the staff into a room and said, "Now folks, I've been informed that there is a request for additional phone reps. Since no one can predict the ups and downs of the business, I do not intend to hire any additional staff. I've never had to lay anyone off yet, and I'm not going to start now. Instead, to help relieve the pressure, I suggest that everyone bring members of their families down to help out as temporary workers."

I called Virginia and asked her to bring some of her friends to the office to help answer the phones. They asked me, "What do we say?"

I answered, "Say hello! And if you don't know the answer to a question, hand your phone over to Frank Raw."

Family, friends and staff all worked together and did their best to fill all the requests.

Chapter 8

STOWERS FINANCIAL ANALYSIS

My objective has always been to try to help people improve their financial positions. I wondered, "What unique idea can I come up with that will truly help people? What will be different from what others are doing? How can our organization stand out?"

It occurred to me that people have no idea how much money it takes today, to provide what they want for their loved ones in the future. They can only guess.

People also have no idea how much money they will have to set aside each month until retirement in order to provide all the income they will need for the rest of their lives. Again, they can only guess.

It occured to me, "Why not write a computer program, that allows for variables, to answer this problem?" The program I wrote originally in 1967 was for a 360 IBM mainframe. We had to use punch cards in order to enter the information into the computer. The original name for the program was Financial Security Analysis.

The analysis determined how much money it would take, in one lump sum, to provide for your loved ones should you die today. It also determined how much money you would need to save each month until retirement in order to provide all the income you might want the rest of your life. The program allowed for many variables to be entered.

This financial analysis program was truly a unique way for our salesmen to help people realize that they could become financially independent.

Chapter 8

PROFILE OF A TEAM MEMBER

BY JACK JONATHAN

When you look at pictures of Jim as a child, or you read his stories about Kemper Military School, it is clear that Jim was a born leader. He is analytical, decisive and determined to do his best. Above all, he wants to help people, and he tries to treat others as he would like to be treated. The founder of one of the most successful mutual fund companies in the country, Jim is:

An unassuming man who, on your first day at work, greets you in his office with a broad smile and an outstretched hand.

The man sitting in the cafeteria with his worn brown bag and peanut butter sandwich, warmly greeting all who go by.

The guy at the company picnic with the camera around his neck delighting in photographing everyone.

One of the guys with his sleeves rolled up, grilling hot dogs at the office picnic.

The dignified, friendly man, standing with his wife, patiently waiting his turn at the barbecue like the rest of the workers, refusing to go to the front of the line.

Chapter 8

These are portraits of Jim the leader who is a team player. A man who believes people work *with* him, not for him. He wants to hear the opinions of all on his team because he truly believes that decisions arrived at as a result of team effort are often the best solutions.

Jim is the kind of leader who really listens to the concerns of the people he works with. His dedication to their well-being is evident in the health program he set up and in his determination to give his people something more meaningful at Christmas than a turkey.

In 1991, there had been an unprecedented record of new accounts flooding support services. True to form, Jim was in the middle of things, helping with every job that needed a hand. An anonymous letter expresses the sentiments of people who have worked with Jim through the years.

Mr. Stowers,

I hope you realize how much you inspire the ground troops who look to you for leadership. The team spirit, the good humor and the unbelievable turnout on Saturday of folks to "get the work done" was something I thought I would never see in American business.

Your own involvement – from recruiting able bodies (and training them in the promised five minutes) to sitting down and processing – certainly set an example that I , for one, was excited to follow.

It becomes easier and easier to see how your are building a large company that feels small.

Photograph by Don Ipock Photography

I was honored to be asked to light the 2002 Olympic flame.

Paul Coker, Jr. cartoon of me blowing out a candle on my peanut butter sandwich on my 80th birthday.

I prefer to use a telephoto lens so that I can catch people by surprise.

That was a good one.

Ready to serve, with Dennis von Waaden!

Here I am at my Yamaha doing one of my favorite things, enjoying my music.

Chapter 9

Taking Off

The Challenger flying over the American Century Towers.

Chapter 9

TAKING OFF

It took many years of absolute determination before our company really began to grow. Along the way, we overcame many obstacles and setbacks, and we solved many problems. Two things stand out that were critical to our success: my fundamental beliefs about investing and my commitment to helping people. I certainly did not enter this business with the idea that I would become wealthy. The business took off because it was based on good investment decisions and a desire to help people succeed. I took no shortcuts.

THE VALUE OF CREATING THE BEST

We had observed several mutual fund complexes become very successful in this new field and we were absolutely confident that we could do that, too. In fact, we were certain that we had built an even better mutual fund complex ourselves. It was the very best, unique and different.

Dear Mr. Stowers:

I truly appreciate the opportunity to work for such a great company! You not only guided the company to a prosperous future, but you created a corporate culture that is among the best. The values and principles with which you live your life are firmly embedded in the foundation of this business. May God bess you on your 80th birthday!

Rob Leach

Chapter 9

The following beliefs and principles about investing contributed to the success of our funds:

The greatest threat to financial security is the loss in the value of a dollar over time. The value of a dollar can decrease by 50 percent every ten years.

The only way to overcome this loss in value is to invest in companies with accelerating earnings and revenues. If there is any question about whether there is true acceleration in a company, we sell it.

*I invest for the long term, and I mean **long** term. The market has proven itself over and over. It goes down, but it always bounces back higher.*

We do not buy industries. We build our portfolios one company at a time.

We work as a team. There is no star manager because our choices are made in terms of the numbers. Any team member who spots a great company, or observes that one of our companies is failing, is responsible for taking action on that security.

We do not speculate with other people's money by trying to time the market.

Chapter 9

HELPING ANYONE TO BECOME
AN INVESTOR

The second pillar of our success was our belief that anyone who was serious about investing would be able to enjoy the fruits of long-term investing. My philosophy of doing business was essential to convincing people that they could trust us to help make their dream of financial independence a reality.

Here are my principles of doing business:

- *Learn what people really want and need.*

- *Determine if we can provide a unique and superior product or service to fill that need.*

- *Do not discount the price of our valuable management or service to anyone.*

- *Never be completely satisfied with what we do.*

- *Always strive to do better.*

- *Try to be unique.*

Investors knew our funds were the best and could help them toward becoming financially independent. To address the challenge of making our image match our investment results and reputation, we needed a logo.

Chapter 9

THE ROCKET LOGO

The first logo of Twentieth Century Investors was designed to denote the modern twentieth century. It had a gold 20th in the middle of a large circle along with a rocket blasting off into space. Our financial reports showed the logo on a background of dark blue with many stars.

After we had used that logo for about ten years, the SEC informed me that the upward pointing rocket in our logo was misleading. It implied that the future direction of the investment results would only be up. If we wanted to continue to use our logo, we had to turn the rocket so its nose pointed down.

I asked why they suddenly came to that conclusion after reviewing this logo over ten years. A staff member ignored my question and pressed the point. I persisted pointing out that a rocket is normally thought to go up.

At this time, Dreyfus Fund had a TV ad showing their Dreyfus lion coming out of a subway exit on Wall Street. I told the SEC staff member, "All right, if you kill the Dreyfus lion and put its feet up in the air, I'll turn that rocket upside down." The conversation stopped. We kept the rocket for a few more years.

**20TH CENTURY
INVESTORS INC.**

Interim logo which was replaced by the oak tree.

Chapter 9

SHARPENING OUR COMPANY IMAGE

You often hear about the importance of location in projecting the correct image. Initially, our office was in the basement of the Country Club Bank located on the Country Club Plaza, one of the first shopping centers in the country. A law firm had previously occupied that space; all of the walls were wood paneled. Visitors were impressed by the solid and traditional appearance the office projected.

As the company grew, we ran out of space. About ten years later, we moved to the third floor on the sunny side of the old Skelly Oil Company building. This move allowed us to keep our location on the wonderful Country

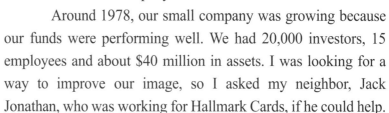

Club Plaza. At that time, we still shared space with Survivors' Benefit Insurance Company.

Around 1978, our small company was growing because our funds were performing well. We had 20,000 investors, 15 employees and about $40 million in assets. I was looking for a way to improve our image, so I asked my neighbor, Jack Jonathan, who was working for Hallmark Cards, if he could help. He was unavailable, but referred me to a small, innovative company, Kuhn & Wittenborn Advertising that could help improve our company image.

Soon after, Whitey Kuhn submitted new designs for our collateral material and over 100 sketches for a new logo to replace the rocket. We finally selected an oak tree because of its strong roots and the length of time it takes to mature. This symbol fits with my philosophy of investing over the long-term and projects the right image to potential investors.

As we became aware of Whitey's abilities, we asked him to help us with a plan that would be a guide for our future growth. The success of our two funds, Growth and Select, caused an avalanche of investors whose orders

Chapter 9

overwhelmed our mailroom. When Whitey was made aware of our problems, he simplified our paperwork and created new standards of quality that were consistent with our image.

GETTING THE WORD OUT WITH ADS

For the first twenty years, our investment record was our best advertisement. As a result, we were fortunate to get some good press in the newspapers and magazines. We eventually decided to begin a campaign to advertise our funds. Our strategy was to use small ads that looked like coupons and required people to mail them back, or call us. Because our funds were such good performers, we received thousands of these coupons and many phone calls.

Still, we wanted to do something even more unique. Whitey came up with the idea of running a strip ad across the bottom of the stocklisting page of *Barron's* magazine. No one had ever done this before. The strip, which was the only ad on the page, cost us the same as a third of a page ad.

In 1986 and 1987, Growth Investors became the #1 fund in the country. Moreover, Growth and Select were the number one and number two mutual funds in all the country. Playing off our success, we created a full-color ad that said, *"Being the number two mutual fund in the country isn't bad, especially when you're also number one."*

Even though our funds were extremely good, they were as vulnerable as all the others when, in October 1987, the market plunged 508 points in one day. Our employees were shaken and there was a feeling of fear and sadness. At the end of the day, I gathered all the people in the company together to encourage them by explaining what had happened.

Chapter 9

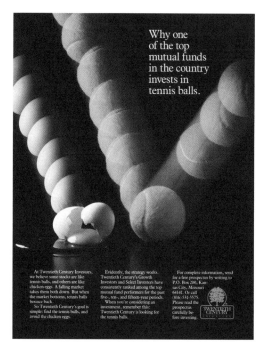

During the meeting, Dennis von Waaden, an officer of the company, climbed a six-foot ladder with an egg in one hand and a tennis ball in the other. Then, with great flair, he dropped them both. The egg splattered on impact and the tennis ball bounced up. This was a dramatic illustration of my point that a strong, high-quality stock (a tennis ball) will accelerate upward after a sharp drop, while a weak stock (an egg) will splatter.

Later, I was interviewed by a reporter for the *Wall Street Journal* who asked me to explain my investment philosophy. I said, "I look at it this way, I try to select tennis balls and avoid chicken eggs."

The interviewer said, "What do you mean?"

"I choose stocks that act like tennis balls. When the market goes down, all stocks go down. But when the market bottoms out, the tennis ball

Chapter 9

stocks hit the bottom and bounce back rapidly. However, stocks that are chicken eggs hit the bottom and splatter."

The reporter was extremely intrigued by my answer and wrote about it in his article. After that, there was a lot of talk about chicken eggs and tennis balls.

In 1988, Kuhn & Wittenborn Advertising created a striking visual image of a tennis ball in motion and a splattered egg. It was our first full-page color ad. We ran it in *Money* magazine, *Changing Times*, *Forbes* and newspapers. This ad was so effective, we also did a version of it to send to our investors. We wanted to reinforce in our investors' minds the importance of staying invested at all times and not trying to time the market.

THE VALUE OF TEAMWORK

Initially, there were only three of us in the company. Whenever we had a problem, we got together; discussed the pros and cons; considered what the consequences would be if we followed each suggestion; and then made a decision.

Over time, I became more and more convinced that decisions arrived at as a result of team discussions were more valuable than those made by individuals. No one person alone would have been able to come up with the ideas stimulated by the group. Although it may seem that team decisions take longer to make, unique solutions are more likely to be arrived at by a team.

As our company grew, we continued to use this team approach. However, for it to be most effective, we needed to attract people who excelled in their field and enjoyed working together toward a shared goal. There was absolutely no place for a *prima donna*, because a team cannot win unless all the members pull in the same direction. Our stars were rewarded for their *cooperative* talents – not for their *competitive* ones.

Chapter 9

Mountains can be moved by an absolutely determined group of outstanding people working together as a team.

It is fun to have people around me who are passionate about the ideas and dreams that excite me. Working together with such a team of people, all focused on solving the same problem, can be exhilarating. By approaching each day with a passion for whatever we do, work and play feel the same.

WHY IS A TEAM SO POWERFUL?

To be able to understand the strength of a group decision, you have to witness the debate about the issues *prior* to the decision. The first rule of being a good team member is to be a good listener and to consider carefully the views of others. Complex problems can only be resolved by the cooperative input of each member of the team. Reaching consensus requires patient deliberation. The result of this group effort usually speaks for itself.

The most powerful team, and the one that is the most fun to work with, is the *A* team. Members of the *A* team are people who excel in their own area of expertise and do not believe they know all the answers. The disciplined minds of each of these creative people, focused on solving the same problem, create a powerful tool for decision-making.

Here are the attributes of people who create a powerful *A* team:

Intelligent and open-minded	*Curious and imaginative*
Good listeners	*Willing to open up*
Able to ask good questions	*Respectful of others' opinions*

Chapter 9

What Makes Us Successful? People Like You!

In the fall of 1992, I was extremely fortunate to have been selected as "The Entrepreneur of the Year" by the Henry W. Bloch School of Business and Public Administration at the University of Missouri-Kansas City.

When I accepted the award, what important message did I want to convey to all the people attending the event and dinner? I thought, why not share our sincere message that I personally sign and send to each new person who is invited to work at American Century? It shares our purpose, beliefs and what we stand for. It also outlines our expectations of everyone.

Instead of giving a speech, I read to those assembled our welcome letter.

Dear Susan Smith,

"Welcome to American Century. I am pleased you are joining our team. Since we will be working together, I would like to share some of my feelings about our company with you.

Years ago, I felt there was an outstanding opportunity to help investors become financially independent by providing them with superior investment management. Taking advantage of that opportunity meant earning and maintaining the trust and confidence of investors – by producing strong investment results over time and by providing consistent, high quality service. Accompanying this concept, it has always been my belief that if we make people successful, they will, in turn, make us successful.

I believe a company is a direct reflection of its people. How we are perceived by others is the product of our individual efforts. What you do every day does make a difference.

Chapter 9

Our long-term success is ultimately linked to your professional growth and development, and to the value we all place on each other. I feel that we must treat each other fairly, with dignity and respect. Beyond this, we seek to provide you with challenging goals; a pleasant work environment; ongoing training; and advanced equipment and technology.

We work together as a team, focusing our energy and our efforts in the same direction toward common goals. We are only as strong as the people with whom we work. Through teamwork, we believe we can achieve consistent results and make better business decisions.

What we expect from you is that you sincerely try to do your very best in all that you do. No one can expect more. We want you to be proud of what you do and what we all do together.

You are considered an individual, not an employee. You will work with us, not for us. You add something unique to American Century – it is the reason we asked you to join our team. Your individual skills and your commitment to excellence make you special – and will help make us special.

Our company has prospered under my fundamental attitude of optimism for the future. As we go forward, I hope you will share with me my belief, "The Best is Yet to Be."

This innovative approach to welcoming our new hires was met with a spontaneous standing ovation.

Chapter 9

CELEBRATING THE PEOPLE WHO MAKE US SUCCESSFUL

The tradition of hiring the very best people is at the core of why we have continued to be so successful. My question to people who join us for the first time at American Century is, "Do you know what makes us successful?" Then I answer with a resounding, **"People like you!"**

It has always been my belief that if we make people successful, they will, in turn, make us successful. From the early beginnings of Stowers & Company, Frank Raw was my inspiration. His amazing qualities and dedication became the standard by which we measure people who join the company.

Frank Raw receiving the first Frank Raw award from me, November 1984.

To honor Frank and to inspire others in the firm to strive to be like him, we established the Francis J. Raw Award. On November 27, 1984, around the time of his 83rd birthday, I presented the first award to Frank.

Since then, we have recognized those people among us who best exemplify the qualities of Frank. These individuals have reached a high level of excellence in their performance and professionalism. They also demonstrate the qualities, character and attitude of Frank: a positive attitude, warm and inviting, optimistic, appreciative and determined to make a difference.

In 1990, we created the Leadership award, which was renamed the James E. Stowers, Jr. award in 2005.

Chapter 9

This award recognizes an individual who brings to life the American Century Leadership Model. Recipients inspire others, create learning environments, communicate effectively and have the courage to be different.

The James E. Stowers, Jr. award is presented annually, along with the Francis Raw award, at the Recognition Celebration which is held in February. American Century has created other awards to recognize those people in the company who have demonstrated the values of our Guiding Principles:

Provide value for our investors.

Challenge and inspire the best people.

Help build a financially sound company.

Are adaptable and innovative.

Work with integrity.

In the March/April 2006 edition of our in-house magazine, *Centurion*, Bill Lyons, American Century Investors President and CEO, was quoted as saying, "Hollywood celebrates acting, but we celebrate values … and the people who exemplify those values in their daily work."

FROM PRIVATELY RUN COMPANY TO PROFESSIONAL MANAGEMENT

As the founder of 20th Century, I had the skills and determination to establish a successful business. I was convinced that if we offered good investment results and provided excellent services, people would want to invest in our mutual funds. However, in 1987, as we reached $5 billion in assets, I wanted to improve our ability to manage our growth while maintaining our innovative excitement. It seemed that the time was right to consider the possibility of formal planning and professional management.

Chapter 9

In 1988, we invited Dr. Eric Flamholtz, a professor from the John Anderson Graduate School of Management at UCLA, to help us make a smooth transition to a professionally managed mutual fund business. Eric had a unique framework for understanding the "growing pains" of our type of company. He helped develop a plan to ensure our orderly growth into a larger business.

On a personal level, I wanted Dr. Flamholtz's help dealing with how to prepare the company for the transition from my leadership to that of the next generation. It is extremely difficult for a founder to let go of the company he has carefully nurtured from its infancy. Dr. Flamholz advised me about how to gradually let go of the responsibilities of CEO.

Our new brand logo, introduced in 1998.

EXPANDING OUR INVESTORS' OPTIONS

We continued to expand our family of funds. Each growth fund was created on my strong belief that the best place to make investments was in companies with accelerating earnings and revenues. By 1994, ninety percent of our funds were in equity stocks and only 10 percent were in investments pegged to the dollar, such as US government bonds, municipal bonds and money market funds.

As our family of funds expanded, so did our way of reaching out to investors. We not only offered our funds directly to investors, we also offered them to financial planners and financial institutions, such as banks and insurance companies.

We felt a need to expand the range of financial instruments we could offer to our investors. In early 1995, we discovered a fund family we thought

Chapter 9

would be a good balance to what we already offered – Benham Funds. They were 90 percent invested in fixed income instruments like money market funds and bond funds. A *USA Today* article called our merger, "A mutual fund marriage of opposites."

James Benham, founder and chairman of Benham Management International, Inc. of Mountain View, California, began his business like I did, by focusing on the small investor. With the acquisition of the Benham Funds, we reached $50 billion in assets under management by June of 1996. One phone call gave investors access to a choice of 60 funds ranging from a real estate fund; to a high yield fixed income fund; to our original Growth and Select funds.

As the millennium approached, we felt that the name Twentieth Century Investors no longer symbolized a forward-looking company. In January 1997, with Benham on board, we adopted a new name – American Century Investments. By our 40th anniversary in October of 1998, we had $75 billion in assets under management.

American Century headquarters in Kansas City.

"The best time to plant an oak tree was 20 years ago. The second best time is now."

To the wise investor, the world is a place full of opportunity where dreams can be realized, for "the best is yet to be."

Even the smallest investment holds great potential within, awaiting only time, nourishment and the right place to grow.

Investing requires patience. Those who look for growth too quickly may see their sprouts wither and die, while those who allow time for strong roots to form should see their investments grow and flourish.

Because of natural market cycles, every long-term investment will go through times that are less favorable to growth. But wise investors will keep their roots firmly planted, waiting patiently for the next growth cycle.

As the young investment grows, it thrives on the attention provided by professional management, while regular investments encourage steady growth.

In its own season, the well tended investment grows to maturity. Patient investors are rewarded, knowing that the strength and stability they sought are the natural result of all the work that's gone before.

Chapter 10

Stowers Innovations
Sharing My Ideas

Chapter 10

SHARING MY IDEAS

When we created Twentieth Century Investors in 1958, we shared office space with Survivor's Benefit Insurance Company. We were trying to help people improve their financial positions by offering outstanding mutual funds along with low-cost, pure, life insurance. I wanted to encourage people to search for life insurance policies that offered the most protection for the least amount of money – policies that could be automatically renewed each year until the insured reached age 100.

There was a lot of information I needed to share in order to help people understand the facts about insurance, as well as to help them make more informed financial decisions. I could reach more people by providing a book to help those who were truly curious about life insurance become aware of all the facts and make the right decision for their families.

In 1967, I decided to write a book, *"Why Waste Your Money on Life Insurance?"* We formed our own publishing company, Deer Publishing, in order to produce the book.

In the Preface of this book, I stated:

In writing this book, I have attempted to show you the true value of life insurance and its effect on you and your family. The facts are presented from your standpoint as an individual interested in life insurance. If you take the time necessary to understand these basic facts, you may be able to greatly improve your position financially.

It is not my intention to tell you what you should do about life insurance, but I do feel that it is my obligation to let you know what the facts are. What you do with your money is your decision and yours alone.

Chapter 10

HELPING INVESTORS

Over time, I became convinced that people truly did not understand what they could do to become financially independent. Furthermore, the actions of some of our small investors clearly demonstrated a lack of understanding in the matter of investing in mutual funds. For instance, one person invested $10 in one of the funds, then wrote a letter to the company requesting that out of the $10 investment, $1 be transferred into another fund; and another dollar be placed in a different fund.

When the executive committee heard of this, they thought they could take care of the problem by asking the investor to redeem his investments. I disagreed. I thought that this was our problem. If investors showed a lack of knowledge about how to invest in mutual funds, we should make them aware instead of turning them away. After all, people cannot become financially secure if they are not aware of the facts about money and not aware of what they can do to grow their money.

I asked the executive committee if they would give me time to write a book in order to help people understand money and investments. Reluctantly, they agreed.

When I told Jack Jonathan, who had been a consultant with American Century since 1988, that we were going to write a book about the value of money and investing, he became excited. "Great," he said. "We will use cartoons."

I asked, "Cartoons?"

"Yes," he replied, "humorous illustrations will lighten up the subject."

Jack suggested using Paul Coker, an illustrator for *MAD* magazine with whom he had worked when he was a corporate director at Hallmark Cards.

Chapter 10

When the executive committee heard about the use of cartoons, they had second thoughts. They thought that a book about finance was a serious matter and wanted to protect my image. We agreed it was a serious matter but felt that the subject could be lightened up and made interesting by using humorous illustrations.

We decided to create a facsimile of the first four chapters and then get opinions and suggestions from editors, executives and other interested readers. To our surprise, everyone thought humorous illustrations were a great idea. However, some people did not like our working title, *The Eternal Bull*. From among the other suggested titles we chose, *Yes, You Can... Achieve Financial Independence*.

I had unwavering determination that nothing was going to prevent me from accomplishing my goals...

While writing the book, I thought of my father. Although he had been an extremely successful surgeon and a graduate from Johns Hopkins Medical School, he was absolutely scared of stocks and the stock market. He was so busy in the practice of surgery that he had not taken the time necessary to understand investing. My father died in 1945, but I was determined that if he'd had the opportunity to read my book, he would clearly understand and become comfortable with investing.

The purpose of the book was to make people aware of the facts about investing and help them understand exactly what they could do financially. No effort would be made to tell people what they *should do*. We just hoped to make people aware of what they *could do* and why it might be wise to do it.

Chapter 10

The book would cover a broad range of subjects regarding money management. Our goal was to communicate with people, not impress them. So each subject had to be described clearly in simple language – not the vocabulary of finance.

The information had to be presented in a unique way. The creative approach we chose was to use a number of charts and graphs to provide a visual impact and to help people understand complex questions. For example, in studying the Dow Jones Industrial Average since 1898, some interesting questions would be, "What are the odds of losing money over various periods of time? What are the odds of gaining? What are the risks over various periods of time?" The analysis of this information had never been presented this way. It was truly unique, as was our use of over one hundred humorous illustrations.

After three years of working on the manuscript, the book was finally published by Deer Publishing Company in 1992 and offered by direct mail to Twentieth Century Investors and bookstores. Why did it take so long? Because we used 93 editors and reviewers whose suggestions were essential to the improvement of the book.

Yes, You Can... Achieve Financial Independence received many favorable comments such as, "Why didn't you write this book 30 years ago?" We were really proud of our efforts.

I am signing books at Barnes and Noble in 1992.

Chapter 10

Since 1992, Stowers Innovations has distributed over 120,000 books. As far as we know, no other mutual fund complex has published such a book.

While preparing the 4th edition, in addition to updating the facts and expanding on some of the important concepts, I added an epilogue, *My Message to You*, expressing my views about investing.

STOWERS FINANCIAL ANALYSIS

After writing the first edition of my book, I realized that I could help even more people if I offered the financial analysis tool I had created in 1968. *The Stowers Financial Analysis* was created to help people become aware of how much money it would take to provide for a loved one should they die. It also makes people aware of exactly how much money must be set aside each month until they retire in order to provide the income they want for the rest of their lives. The analysis shows the amount of money required in *today's dollars* to provide what is desired in the future.

The second edition offered the Financial Security Analysis to readers willing to complete a questionnaire in the back of the book and send it in for us to analyze.

When personal computers became commonplace, we saw an opportunity to make the Stowers Financial Analysis even more user friendly. An energetic computer programmer rewrote the program for a PC. When we released the 4th edition of *Yes, You Can... Achieve Financial Independence* in 2004, we included a CD-ROM version of the security analysis.

All of this was done in an effort to make it as easy as possible for people to examine what they truly want in their future and encourage them to make the financial decisions **now** that will help them to become financially independent **later**.

Chapter 10

STOWERS INNOVATIONS, INC.

In the late 1990's, the John Deere Company claimed we were diluting their brand and requested that we change the name of Deer Publishing to something more descriptive.

People think of me as an entrepreneur, but I describe myself as an innovator. Since our company was publishing my concepts and beliefs, we decided on a new, more appropriate name, Stowers Innovations, Inc., a wholly owned subsidiary of American Century Investments.

With this change, we also began to broaden our mission. Although our first book, *Yes, You Can... Achieve Financial Independence*, focused on financial matters, it also emphasized the values and character traits which would help people improve their financial positions.

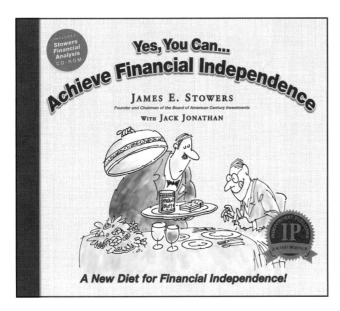

4th Edition with the Stowers Financial Analysis CD ROM

Chapter 10

Our new mission is to provide information that makes people aware of how they can live a meaningful life through an understanding of their values, personal relationships, finances, good physical health and mental well-being.

Since 1992, four editions of *Yes You Can ... Achieve Financial Independence* have been published, as well as four other titles. Additional books in the *Yes, You Can...* series are planned.

In addition to our book series, we also offer:

A CD-ROM version of the Stowers Financial Analysis.

A web site which links Stowers Innovations to American Century.

A quarterly newsletter with seasonally topical articles.

Lunch and Learn sessions and lectures.

In 2005, Stowers Innovations, along with American Century, sponsored Achieve Financial Independence Week™. This annual event; which takes place the third week in October, helps to raise national awareness of the importance of managing money and avoiding debt.

American Century Investments may be the only mutual fund complex offering books to help people improve their financial position and live happier and more fulfilling lives. I am convinced that Stowers Innovations contributes to making American Century Investments unique.

Chapter 10

Stowers Innovations Books

Yes, You Can...

Achieve Financial Independence

Raise Financially Aware Kids

Afford to Raise a Family

Find More Meaning in Your Life

Achieve Financial Harmony

My next book will be, *Yes, You Can... Do More Than You Think You Can: My Treasure Chest.*

Many of us have a treasure chest – a gold mine of ideas and experiences. However, unless we mine our treasure and refine it into a useful form, it loses its value.

In *My Treasure Chest*, I will share the thoughts and ideas that have added value to my life. I hope these treasures will stimulate your thinking and help you, too, improve the quality of your life.

Your future depends on *your* determination to become who *you* want to be.

PART FOUR

Giving Back

I believe that our purpose
in life is to fulfill our potential
and to help others.

A New Meaning for Endowment

BY JACK JONATHAN

*E*ndowment normally refers to a sum of money – capital – that funds a project.

It can also be the qualities of a person whose character and achievements inspire, create and endure beyond their lifetime in something larger than themselves.

Jim Stowers not only endows the Stowers Institute for Medical Research with the means to fund research forever, he also endows it with his qualities of trust, optimism and determination. Those whose lives he has touched feel his power to inspire them to be the best they can be.

Jim's legacy will continue to make its mark on the future health and well-being of people everywhere beyond his lifetime.

Chapter 11

Virginia:
My Lifetime Partner

———

Chapter 11

VIRGINIA: MY LIFETIME PARTNER

One of the keys to my success in business was that I sought out and surrounded myself with the most talented people. Together we created the dynamics needed to make the business grow.

Now I think we're melding together... Jack talks about life being a relay race, but I think Jim and I are now holding the baton together.

Virginia Stowers

However, nothing can compare to my good fortune in marrying Virginia Ann Glascock. Even though a person's character emerges with renewed strength when challenged, I wonder if I could have survived without Virginia. While we sometimes joke about how we first met, I can only say that our relationship, as it developed into a true partnership, made it

possible for me to grow, prosper and finally succeed beyond my expectations.

Before I married Virginia in 1954, I thought very seriously about what "marriage" meant to me. I thought of marriage as a lifetime partnership between a man and woman in love, one not dominated by either partner, sharing their experiences as they went through life.

I realized that I was not perfect, and I did not expect my future wife to be perfect. As a partner, I would have to be willing to fully accept my wife's weaknesses, as she would have to be willing to accept mine. We would enjoy our life together as partners.

Before getting married, I wanted to be sure that the woman I chose absolutely loved me.

Chapter 11

Some people say that a good marriage begins with friendship. However, the day I set eyes on Virginia none of this logic mattered. We first met at a Christmas Party at Research Hospital in 1952. I noticed her sitting with a group of doctors. Gorgeous would not be enough to describe Virginia. What drew me to her was passion, not logic or friendship. I was bold enough to break the ice by trying to entice her to take a bite of my candy cane. Even though she did not take a bite, that was the beginning of our romance.

Virginia's graduation photo.

What I did not know was that Virginia had seen me first. Much later, she confessed that when she first noticed me, she had turned and asked the doctor next to her, "Who is that person? If you find out his name, I will marry him."

***Essential Attributes
of a Good Marriage***

Share responsibilities at home.

Be faithful and loving.

*Find out what your spouse
wants to do.*

Do things your spouse enjoys.

Spend time together.

Be respectful.

Our sentiments had converged across the room. If I had known she had a special feeling for me, too, I would have married her right then. A little more than a year later, on February 4, 1954, Virginia and I were married.

Our married life began with a five-year-old car, a one-bedroom apartment, $1,000, loads of love and the determination that we were going to become financially independent. In the ensuing years, I believe that we have done everything, and I mean everything, that we have truly wanted to do.

Chapter 11

VIRGINIA'S ROOTS

I have found that good friendships are easiest when two people are alike in intellect and interests; financial and cultural backgrounds; and have like family upbringings. This is certainly true of Virginia and me. Clayton Glascock, her father, was a professional man – a pharmacist. Gertrude Francis Wright, her mother, had the privilege of higher education and was a teacher.

Although my mother did not work outside of our home when we were children, she became a very successful businesswoman after my father died. The expectations I had about a marriage partner came largely from those qualities I recognized in my own mother – strength, intelligence, independence and self-reliance. Virginia shares all of these qualities.

Virginia, a pioneer woman.

THE IMPORTANCE OF SELF-RELIANCE

Virginia has been described as "a unique blend of pioneer woman and modern lady." Her self-reliance was an important factor in our being able to marry when we did. We were still dating when I was trying to decide whether I should leave medicine.

We talked about getting married, but Jim said, "I do not have a way of earning a living, yet. Maybe we should wait."

Chapter 11

I replied, "I'm working, so it won't make any difference. If you want to go ahead and get married, I'm right behind you."
Virginia

Even after we had children, Virginia continued to work. We lived off my income and invested hers. It was her patience and support through countless early struggles that helped me stay focused on the goal of achieving financial independence.

I had always wanted to be a nurse. I had a calling for it – several relatives were nurses or in the medical profession. When I thought about specializing in anesthesia, Jim encouraged me, "I think you'll do real well at that." Anesthesia was a good specialty for a wife and mother. I think everyone should get away from her family once in a while, take a deep breath and say, "Who am I?" I had someone very reliable to help with the children.
Virginia

Like my father, I found myself very focused on my career. It took a lot of emotional and physical energy to learn about my new career, develop the business and overcome setbacks. Virginia's capable running of our home was crucial to my being able to have the time to build the business and still enjoy the pleasures of family life.

Many fathers who work hard to support their family miss out on the joys of seeing their children grow up. As a result, they may never feel close to their children. I am grateful to Virginia for transmitting her respect and appreciation for me to the children. They, in turn, echoed their mother and grew up loving and respecting me. I feel fortunate to have good relationships with all my children and their spouses.

Chapter 11

PARTNER

Virginia complements and is an essential partner in our marriage. Although when we first married, she did not know a great deal about finances, she agreed with me about the importance of becoming financially independent. She quickly learned how to make good financial decisions.

The Fur Coat

As newlyweds, our entertainment was walking and window shopping.

One winter day, as we walked by an exclusive fur store, we stopped and admired one of the beautiful fur coats. I asked Virginia if she wanted it. She said she really did, but then added, "But we can't afford it because it would reduce our investment savings."

We continued on our walk.

A year or so later, after we had saved some money, we happened to walk by the same store. Again we stopped to admire the beautiful coats. I asked Virginia if she wanted one of them. This time Virginia didn't answer me right away. Finally she said, "No, I don't want one."

I asked why. She continued, "If I had one, I would lose the earnings on the money it would take to buy the coat. I would also have to pay for insurance and storage. No, I would rather have my money working for me."

This story is typical of how careful Virginia is about getting her money's worth. I sometimes think that she is even more frugal than I am.

Virginia and I did not win the lottery. We were just determined to invest every penny we could. It was a great help that Virginia had a career she loved and was happy to live off my salary, putting her money away for investing and saving.

Chapter 11

We had four children in six years, and yet, until 1986, when I was being treated for cancer, Virginia continued to work. Fortunately, she has superior homemaking skills and is very efficient. She is an excellent cook and she can sew everything from dresses for our daughters and herself, to men's shirts and even household items like draperies.

When I think about it now, it is remarkable how seamlessly she seemed to move from nurturing our children and caring for our home, to working in anesthesia at Research or Menorah Hospitals.

Pamela, our first child.

Virginia has been asked why she did not help me in the business. She did help out with the business when I really needed her. However, her greatest support was her ability to manage our home and family with so much love and care.

I am so fortunate that Virginia was willing to learn about the value of money and that we came to have the same point of view. This meeting of the minds has made our marriage harmonious.

The supreme happiness in life
is the conviction that we are loved.

Victor Hugo

Chapter 11

MY CHAMPION

Virginia is not just a good partner at home. She understands me and supports my interests. For example, I wanted to go back on active duty with the Air Force to learn how to pilot a jet. This meant I would have to spend a little over a month at Craig Air Force Base in Selma, Alabama, for jet transition training.

In the fifties, flying was quite a novelty. Some women would have been upset if their husband wanted to fly, but not Virginia. She knew it was my dream to fly jets. So she was supportive of me going back on active duty.

Virginia, Chairman of the Board of the Stowers family, with me at the controls of the Global Express.

Jim called from Craig to say, "I am flying to Kansas City, can you pick me up?"

I said, "Sure."

I got the baby into the car and drove twenty miles out to Richards Gebaur Air Force Base to pick him up. I was shocked, Jim had already landed.

Jim returned to the Air Force Reserve and flew on weekends to keep up his flying skills.

Virginia

I have Virginia to thank for helping me build American Century Investments into what it is today. Building a business is an up and down affair. There were setbacks in growing the mutual fund business. It was so comforting to always have Virginia there to encourage me, contribute to our savings plan and even to work at the business occasionally.

Chapter 11

Once, at a meeting with important consultants, we sat around a table with Virginia on my right. It was suggested that we introduce ourselves. Starting at the far end of the table, people stated their name and their title, such as officer or director. When it was Virginia's turn, she informed everyone,

"I am Virginia Stowers, the Chairman of the Board of the Stowers family." Everyone laughed.

I asked her "Why did you say that?"

She answered, "Because I am."

Virginia sincerely believes in me and has the utmost confidence in my abilities. I question whether I could have accomplished all that I have without her continued encouragement. The lion's share of the credit for my accomplishments must go to Virginia, who has always been patient and supportive through countless events along the way.

Virginia truly is a great woman, wife and partner.

MELDING TOGETHER

In 1987, when I was diagnosed with cancer, Virginia stopped working as a nurse to support me through my treatment and healing. Later, she and our daughter, Kathy, were also diagnosed with cancer and went through treatment and recovery. Instead of retiring from the world, Virginia put her energy into helping others in the community through her work at the Rose Brooks Center for battered women and their children. Today she is also active in supporting the Center for Practical Bioethics.

Chapter 11

Virginia and me, partners in planning at the site of the future Stowers Institute for Medical Research.

OUR BIG DREAM

One of the most exciting ventures of our marriage came in August of 1994, when Virginia and I decided to form the Stowers Institute for Medical Research. Here our medical interests, my expertise in finance and our shared sense of optimism, came together to help us give back to the community in a way that can really make a difference.

Now, I think we're melding together. Before, Jim seemed to be always charging ahead of me on new projects, but now I am catching up, and we are coming together with our interest in the Stowers Institute. I am convinced that our scientists at the Institute will be able to find the cures for diseases such as Parkinson's, and traumas such as spinal cord injuries. Jack talks about life being a relay race, but I think Jim and I are now holding the baton together.

Virginia

Chapter 11

FAMILY TRIBUTE

There is no more fitting ending to this chapter than the tribute our children wrote for Virginia in 1999, when they nominated her to be recognized by the Women's Foundation of Greater Kansas City.

"You are not only proof that behind every successful man there's a great woman, but that behind a great woman stands a deeply appreciative husband, as well as children and their families.

You are teacher, confidante and best friend … holding the family together in times of change and stress.

For all these things and many more, you've earned your title as "Chairman of the Board of the Stowers family."

A family gathering in 2006. Virginia and I surrounded by all of our children and three of our five grandchildren.

Birth of the Stowers Institute for Medical Research

Reaching through the rock of adversity

to the well-spring of hope.

Chapter 12

*Jim and Virginia are so purely motivated to do good things,
that their enterprise seems to attract an extraordinary degree of
good fortune that helps it all along.*

Bill Neaves
President and CEO, Stowers Institute for Medical Research

THROUGH TEARS COMES A VISION

Because of my father's early death, I was determined to live a healthy life and to help people who worked for my company become aware of what they could do to remain healthy. In 1986, American Century sponsored its first complete blood screening for all of its people. It screened the hematology, blood chemistries, cardiac risk, thyroid panel and tumor marker panel.

My results were all normal.

In January of 1987, when I was 63 years old, I was examined by my doctor during a routine physical. At that time, I was concerned that I might have a heart problem because my father had died at the age of 55 from a heart attack. After his examination, the doctor informed me that he had found a nodule on my prostate and suggested that I look further into it.

From my medical training, I realized that I had cancer of the prostate. This surprised me because the tumor markers on my comprehensive blood test did not indicate a problem. My doctor asked me which tumor marker was run. I said it was Prostatic Acid Phosphatase (PAP). He replied "Oh, that only tests if cancer has metastasized to bone. You should have used Prostate Specific Antigen (PSA)."

Today, American Century offers employees the option to choose which markers are run, including PSA.

Chapter 12

I was not scared that I had cancer, but I was tremendously concerned that I might receive the wrong treatment, which could be fatal. I was fortunate to find the right doctor. He removed my prostate, eliminating the cancer from my body.

THE STOWERS FOUNDATION

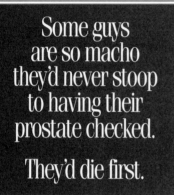

During my recovery period, my doctor asked if I would help him acquire a certain piece of laboratory equipment for $10,000. Rather than giving money that would be instantly spent, even for a worthy cause, I felt I could help this cause better if I established an endowment as seed money.

The Stowers Foundation was established in 1988. At that time, Virginia and I wanted to make people aware that, for early detection of prostate cancer, every man should have a rectal exam. I was hopeful that, by getting the word out about prostate cancer, we could help save lives. By 1994, the foundation had funded about 8,000 free prostate screenings at St. Luke's Hospital.

To help teach doctors how to medically and surgically treat prostate cancer, we set up a one-year fellowship program in clinical research on urologic cancer. Each year we invited one or two specialists to come to Kansas City.

Chapter 12

BROADENING OUR VISION

In 1993, Virginia was diagnosed with breast cancer. Later, our daughter, Kathy, also battled cancer. Like me, they were able to get the right doctor and the right treatment and have remained cancer free.

Only someone who has been told that they have cancer can describe the fear, sadness and loneliness those words can bring. You learn that you are not indestructible. Virginia found that, "Cancer teaches you not to waste time fretting about small things. You learn to focus on the most significant things in life."

Dream lofty dreams, and as you dream, so shall you become. Your vision is the promise of what you shall at last unveil.
John Ruskin

We asked ourselves, "How can we improve the quality of others lives so they, too, can continue to enjoy what they have?" We wanted to give back something more valuable than money to the millions of people who made our success possible. What meaningful action could we take? Was there a universal cause around which everyone could rally?

After a great deal of thought, we decided to dedicate our resources to creating the most innovative and effective medical research institute in the world. To do so, we were determined to apply to our new venture the same values, discipline and imagination that had made American Century so successful.

Chapter 12

THE KITCHEN CABINET

It is easy for someone who is not informed to give money away and see it go to waste because they did not have adequate information. We knew we could not realize our dream alone. Furthermore, I have always believed that a decision arrived at as a result of team discussions is better than the one made by an individual.

During the spring of 1994, we began our discovery process by forming an advisory group to appraise various scientific approaches used by some of the most prestigious research institutions and biotechnology companies. This first advisory board, our "Kitchen Cabinet," consisted of people from a variety of professions: medical, legal, business, creative, education and research. At first, we invited people we knew in Kansas City, some of whom had been on the board of the *Stowers Foundation*.

In July of 1994, the Kitchen Cabinet met to plan the mission and goals of the Stowers Institute for Medical Research so that it could really make a difference. After a thorough study of the IRS law, we established the Stowers Institute for Medical Research as a Medical Research Organization (MRO), a public charity.

MRO Requirements

- *The organization is required to be directly engaged in the continuous active conduct of medical research in conjunction with a hospital.*

- *If the organization annually spends 3.5 percent or more of the fair market value of its endowment in the continuous active conduct of medical research, the above requirement will be satisfied.*

Chapter 12

Cartoon from KC Business Journal, March 6-12, 1998.

GETTING EDUCATED

We discussed our vision with local business leaders. We then spent time visiting various medical research institutions to learn more about how to conduct scientific research.

One of the places we visited was the Howard Hughes Medical Institute in Maryland, created by the late Howard Hughes. They finance scientists in laboratories all over the country, several of whom are Nobel Prize winners. Although they are the gold standard for medical research, our long-term vision was to have our researchers work as a team in one location.

Chapter 12

We also visited the excellent Rockefeller Institute in New York City. They suggested that our money would be better off invested in their organization. However, we were confident that we could do a better job ourselves and politely rejected their proposal.

One of their scientists asked me which kind of scientific research we planned to do: *basic*, *applied* or *clinical*.

We realized we needed to educate ourselves about the kind of research organization we wanted to set up. There was much work to be done.

Which sites should we visit, and who should we consult with?

How would we fund our organization?

Should we solicit public support?

What should our research focus be?

Where should we build our research campus?

What elements should we build into our laboratories?

How do we attract the very best scientists?

First Kitchen Cabinet

Arthur Brand	*Whitey Kuhn*	*Nathan Stark*
Richard Brown	*Jack Jonathan*	*Jim Stowers, Jr.*
Mary Cooksey	*Robert McNealy*	*Byron Thompson*
Laurie Doane	*Robert Pearson*	*David Welte*

The Institute will be an absolutely special place. M.D. Anderson made a difference in Houston. Mayo made a difference in Rochester. And we want to make a difference right here in Kansas City.

From an interview in Ingrams Magazine,
December, 1994.

Chapter 12

RESEARCH SCIENTISTS

Each of the scientists we met helped us to understand more about scientific research. One researcher told us not to expect anything from science except publications. I heard that comment loud and clear. If we attract the very best, I want scientific discoveries in addition to publications.

Our scientists have dreamed for years of an institution of independent scientists, working together not as subordinates of some great executive officer, but joined by the desire, indeed by the spiritual necessity, to understand the origin of life, and to help one another with their individual understanding.

From *Cybernetics* by Norbert Weiner, 1948

Bob Stout, Ph.D., a prominent microbiologist at Clinical Reference Lab in Kansas City, helped explain science to us. He said many scientists think that most of the answers to scientific problems are to be found in only their specialty. However, Bob, who had studied several disciplines while at UCLA, realized that scientific problems can best be solved when different disciplines work together. He knew of Lee Hood, Ph.D., the William Gates III Professor of Molecular Biotechnology at the University of Washington, who practiced this interdisciplinary approach to science.

We met with Dr. Hood and informed him about the Institute, its organization and what it was trying to do. Lee asked, "What kind of science do you intend to do, *science* or *cutting edge science*?

I answered, "If the Institute does not intend to do cutting edge science, I do not want to do any science."

Dr. Lee Hood became the chairman of the Scientific Advisory Board for the Institute. He later added four more scientists to the advisory board who

Chapter 12

are internationally recognized members of the National Academy of Sciences: Eric Davidson, from Cal Tech; Eric N. Olson, from the University of Texas; Michael S. Levine, from Berkeley; and Douglas A. Melton, from Harvard.

RESEARCH FOCUS

There were many passionate discussions during the Kitchen Cabinet meetings as we considered the question of whether we should focus on basic research, or research with direct commercial or clinical applications. Since we were determined to do cutting edge science in order to discover the causes of diseases and the means to prevent them, we eventually came to a consensus that the Stowers Institute should be dedicated to basic research.

Research in basic science has made possible much of the 20th century's improvement in health care and general well-being, as well as our country's economic growth. Unfortunately, in this era when business and industry are primarily interested in financing research for commercial purposes, basic research is not receiving the attention it should.

We were fascinated by the concept of bringing together the powerful fields of biology, chemistry, computer science, engineering, mathematics and physics to analyze and understand complex biological challenges. This cross-disciplinary approach made sense to us.

As a society, we are shirking our support for basic science at the very time when our previous support is reaping great returns. In doing so, we jeopardize not only our legacy of scientific achievement, but also the economic prosperity of the near future.

Nathan Myhrvold of Microsoft
in *Science*, 1998

213

Chapter 12

We wanted the work of the Stowers Institute to focus on the unique, strongly held scientific vision that everything in life is influenced by genetic systems and the manner in which their activity is regulated and controlled.

GETTING STARTED

Before the Institute could open its doors, we needed to have an income available to provide for a minimum number of laboratories required for an effective research center. How could we perform scientific research having an endowment worth only $50,000,000?

We asked our Scientific Advisory Board how much money was needed each year for a good scientific research program. They estimated that $14,000,000 would be needed each year. That figure really shocked me at the time. Receiving 3.5 percent on a $50,000,000 endowment would produce only $1,750,000 a year.

I informed the Scientific Advisory Board we only had $1,750,000 to spend. They said no, you really have $50,000,000 to spend. I answered, "You truly don't understand. We are not going to spend any part of the seed that produces the income. We are absolutely determined not to spend more than 3.5 percent of the endowment each year."

From the figures provided by the Scientific Advisory Board, it was clear that we needed an initial endowment of at least $400 million dollars to start the laboratories, provide economic stability and assure well-funded future research.

Chapter 12

OUR MISSION STATEMENT

To make a significant contribution to humanity through medical research, by expanding our understanding of the secrets of life and by improving life's quality through innovative approaches to the causes, treatment and prevention of diseases.

THE CONSORTIUM

How could we provide for the MRO expenditure requirements of using 3.5 percent of the endowment for research every year? Given our small endowment, it made sense to use our limited resources to initiate our research mission in the form of a consortium.

Our first consortium consisted of four laboratories: Lee Hood's lab at University of Washington, two labs at Cal Tech with Eric Davidson and the McLaughlin Research Institute in Great Falls, Montana. These four labs worked together as an integral team, with each focusing on a different problem in the complex issues of gene regulation or expression.

The consortium was a start. However, in the long run, we felt that our mission would be best served if our scientists were housed in one location where they could easily communicate and collaborate with each other. We also knew that the best scientists would be drawn to us by spacious state-of-the art laboratories, the latest equipment, good lab support and outstanding core facilities.

Chapter 12

A Fantastic Discovery to Fund Scientific Research

We were faced with a dilemma. How could we raise our endowment to accomplish our mission? An investment professional, John Latshaw, who was helping us write the prospectus for the Institute, asked, "If someone offered to pay $350 million to receive all of the scientific discoveries ever discovered by the scientists of the Institute, would you accept that offer?"

I thought a few minutes and answered, "Sure, provided they would be willing to give 50 percent of all the profits to the scientists who made the discovery."

He answered, "Then why don't you do that?"

That one thought convinced me it was absolutely possible to greatly leverage the future value of all the scientific breakthroughs that would be discovered by the Institute.

JP Morgan Buys Shares in American Century

In January of 1998, while we were considering how to implement John Latshaw's idea, J.P. Morgan & Company, the 150-year-old bank holding firm of New York City, negotiated with management of American Century Companies to buy 45 percent of its common stock. Virginia and I had contributed a small amount of our common stock holdings to the Institute that was later sold to J.P. Morgan for $300 million.

Chapter 12

Invested carefully, that initial endowment should average a healthy rate of growth. Dedicating 3.5 percent of that investment each year to scientific research and administration would enable us to spend about $12 million the first year and more as the value of the endowment grew. That large sum of money was relatively modest when compared to the cost of staffing and equipping a first-rate scientific laboratory. With that level of support, we felt that we would be able to initiate research in Kansas City by the year 2000.

An interviewer from Forbes magazine asked, "What did you do when J.P. Morgan bought the $900 million worth of American Century stock?"

I replied, "What do you mean, what did I do?"

The interviewer asked, "Did you go out and buy a BMW?"

I said, "No, we went out to dinner."

A MAJOR RESEARCH CENTER IN KANSAS CITY?

From the very beginning, our intention was to use the discoveries of the Stowers Institute for Medical Research to kick-start an entire biotechnology sector in Kansas City. We expected that a multi-billion dollar industry would grow here over the next several decades. Yet, despite the advantages for scientists, we constantly heard doubts about our determination to build this world-class research center in the Midwest.

Chapter 12

Bringing the Best Science to KC

From an interview in the *Kansas City Business Journal*. February 27 – March 5, 1998

Dan Balaban: *There are some skeptics who say the project won't work in Kansas City, that you can't cause a world-renowned medical research center to simply rise from the plains. Why not endow an established research center such as MD Anderson or Rockefeller University?*

Jim: *Goldman Sachs said we couldn't do it in Kansas City, we would have to go to the coasts. I said, "Time out. I want it here! My roots go back to the founding fathers of this city. This is my home."*

There are many reasons why the Stowers Institute should be in Kansas City. To name a few:

My family roots extend to the founding fathers of Kansas City 200 years ago.

I started Twentieth Century nearly 50 years ago in the basement of a bank on the Country Club Plaza in Kansas City. It now employs over 2,000 people and is estimated to bring $560 million a year to the local economy.

The Stowers Institute can become a world renowned center for medical research, one that will always be financially self-sufficient.

We may lack the critical mass of scientists in the metropolitan area. But why not Kansas City? Was Kansas City known 50 years ago as the home of one of the top five mutual funds in the United States?

Finally, my wife and I want to give back something more valuable than money to all the people who have made our success possible.

Chapter 12

An overview of the Stowers Institute Campus.

We are committed to making Kansas City one of the leading
biomedical research centers in the world!

Chapter 12

A HOME FOR THE INSTITUTE

We were determined to absolutely 'WOW' the best scientists, our community and the world with the quality of our facilities. The research laboratories we saw that had been established for Nobel Prize laureates averaged between 6,000 and 8,000 square feet. We heard repeatedly that a "star" investigator would be drawn to us by the size of our laboratories, the quality of laboratory support and the freedom to conduct research. Their salary would be secondary!

At one of our Kitchen Cabinet board meetings concerning this subject, one member suggested the Institute start out by building a 25,000 square foot lab on the University of Missouri-Kansas City campus.

I raised the question, "Would a building of this size absolutely 'WOW' the scientists, our community or the world? Would people be convinced of our determination to be a success?"

I said that I wanted to have a lot of brick and mortar available to convince people that we were truly serious.

An Opportunity

A major 600,000 square foot hospital had recently moved from a 10-acre plot of land directly across from University of Missouri-Kansas City to a new location in the city. The Institute was able to negotiate an agreement to buy the hospital, a 600 car parking structure and a four-story doctors' office building on that 10-acre plot of land for approximately $10,000,000.

Chapter 12

We decided to finance the purchase, renovation and construction of the Institute's Kansas City headquarters by issuing tax-exempt revenue bonds underwritten by J.P. Morgan. In doing so, we could build the campus and furnish it with sophisticated scientific equipment without taking anything away from the scientific research.

IF YOU BUILD IT, THEY WILL COME

When we visited various research institutions, we realized the importance of adequate facilities. Our goal was to provide the Institute's scientists with the most desirable facilities in which to make their discoveries. Having adequate space and the most powerful, sophisticated tools would allow them to pursue the life-giving answers we are all seeking.

Finally, after much preparation, we began construction of the Stowers Institute. J.E. Dunn Construction Co. of Kansas City was the general contractor. The general architect, with primary responsibility for the exterior and overall design, was the Kansas City firm of Peckham Guyton Albers & Viets. MBT Architecture of San Francisco, one of the few architectural firms in the country specializing in research facilities, designed the laboratory spaces and other areas related to research.

Our instructions were simple: Create the very best. We wanted the ten-acre campus to be an environment that inspires creative research and speeds discoveries.

We had an annual Scientific Advisory Board meeting at the campus before the buildings were completed. We gave the advisory board a tour of the uncompleted buildings. They were extremely impressed.

As we were walking on the tour, Michael S. Levine, Ph.D. shouted loudly so everyone could hear, "If you build it, they will come."

Chapter 12

The interior was the responsibility of my wife, Virginia. Because we believe it is important for scientists to work together in a setting conducive to interaction and collaboration, Virginia definitely did not want a sterile, scientific atmosphere. She was determined to achieve a warm feeling to honor the people and the work they would be doing.

We visited with each member of the Institute's Scientific Advisory Board and asked what they liked and disliked about their own lab. Each was asked what would make their lab truly great. All of the answers were tabulated and given to the architects. One of their requests was to include a large state-of-the-art animal facility.

BUILDING THE VERY BEST

While the Institute's campus was being built, the construction superintendent asked if I could come up with some guiding principles to inspire and motivate all the workers. I wrote down some of the principles that have guided my life. These were made into signs that were displayed around the construction site. The workers were inspired and believed they had been given the opportunity to build a fantastic research campus. They were extremely proud and wanted to be remembered for their part in this effort.

Soon after the campus was finished, our interior architect saw me standing outside the administration building and asked, "Isn't this great?" I asked him what he meant. He said, "When I design lab buildings, I do my very best to create outstanding designs, but clients

> **BUILDERS GUIDING PRINCIPLES**
>
> Do it right the first time.
>
> Do your very best at whatever you do.
>
> Be extremely proud of what you do.
>
> What you do really does make a difference.
>
> You will be remembered forever for what you do.
>
> You will be part of the team that made it happen.

Construction Site Sign.

Chapter 12

usually eliminate many of the features in order to save money. You didn't take out any features, and it sure shows." I thought that was a fantastic compliment.

The planning, dedication, time and energy spent by the architects and the thousands of gifted craftsmen that helped build this magnificent research institute was a true labor of love: a "Hope for Life" and the future of mankind.

OUR MANAGEMENT TEAM

Stowers Institute for Medical Research will be a great success only with a management team of extremely outstanding people. A member of our Scientific Advisory Board, Eric N. Olson, Ph.D., highly recommended we meet an outstanding scientist, William B. Neaves, Ph.D., Dean of the University of Texas Southwestern Medical Center in Dallas, Texas. We were extremely impressed with him and his beliefs and

In February of 2000, I said, "Jim, if you're ready for action rather than advice, I can think of nothing I'd rather do than join your team and help you launch this."

Bill Neaves

we invited him to be one of our advisors. Three years later, we were delighted and surprised when he asked us if he could be the president and CEO of the Institute.

As we were searching for a scientist to become the director of the Institute, another member of our Scientific Advisory Board, Eric Davidson, Ph.D., suggested that we meet Robb E. Krumlauf, Ph.D., who for the past 15 years had been at the National Institute for Medical Research at Mill Hill, London. After meeting with him in Kansas City, we were convinced that we would like to have this outstanding scientist join us.

Chapter 12

The Chairman of our Scientific Advisory Board, Lee Hood, Ph.D., resigned from the Board to focus his energy on his own research organization in Seattle. We deeply appreciate all that he did for us.

We are also fortunate that an existing member of the board accepted the invitation of Bill Neaves to become the new Chairman of the Scientific Advisory Board. Doug Melton agreed to serve under the condition that the appointment of every principal investigator would be approved by all the members of the Board.

The make up of the Scientific Advisory Board is as follows:

Doug Melton, Ph.D.
> Chairman of the Scientific Advisory Board
> Harvard University and Investigator
> of the Howard Hughes Medical Institute

Michael S. Levine, Ph.D.
> University of California-Berkeley

Susan L. Lindquist, Ph.D.
> Massachusetts Institute of Technology

Eric N. Olson, Ph.D.
> University of Texas Southwestern Medical Center

Janet Rossant, Ph.D.
> University of Toronto

Joshua Sanes, Ph.D.
> Harvard University

Charles J. Sherr, M.D., Ph.D.
> St. Jude Children's Research Hospital and Investigator
> of the Howard Hughes Medical Institute

Chapter 12

ATTRACTING THE VERY BEST SCIENTISTS TO KANSAS CITY

I was absolutely convinced that if the Stowers Institute did not attract the very best, its success would be purely accidental.

The Institute must "raise the bar" and invite only the very best scientists to enter, and those people must welcome working together as a team. We were told that if the bar is lowered just once, the Institute could severely damage its reputation.

It would be rather easy to pick only great scientists whose best work was behind them. There's no risk in that. The proof of the value of their work has already been demonstrated. But it would hardly be ground breaking, and it would hardly be satisfying to use the superb resources that Jim and Virginia provided to simply assemble a group of established stars, whose best work was behind them.

So in the spirit of wanting to use those resources to do really novel things, things that had not been done before, important things that might, in fact, be very difficult to do in a different environment, it was really critical to get people whose best work was ahead of them.

Bill Neaves

We were determined to offer a luxury most scientists can only dream of: an opportunity to put all their effort into their research. All the funding would be provided in perpetuity and the scientists would not have to spend half their time writing grants to please the current politically-correct scientific research focus. In short, they could passionately pursue their work and have a chance to create major breakthroughs. Furthermore, if any of their discoveries made a profit, they would receive 50 percent of those profits.

Chapter 12

I have always strongly believed in the importance of investing in the very best, state-of-the-art technology. Bill Neaves agreed with me.

Other advantages offered to our scientists are:

The Institute's reputation as a premiere research facility.

The Institute's passion for excellence and desire to make a difference.

An opportunity to work closely with other outstanding scientists.

The sincerity of the Institute's management.

The quality of life in Kansas City, which along with its many cultural events, includes being a great place to raise a family.

Lack of bureaucracy.

FUNDING: ENDOWMENT-BASED SCIENTIFIC RESEARCH

Most research organizations receive money for their scientific efforts in the form of grants from the government, pharmaceutical companies and private sources. Sadly, many scientists currently devote 50 percent or more of their time searching and applying for funding. If the search for money begins to outweigh the precious time for vital research, it is a tragic waste of scarce resources – the scientists' talents.

The Stowers Institute is different because it is financially independent. Our scientists have the advantage of dedicating all their efforts to achieving scientific breakthroughs. Scientists are compromised by political influences when they are not independently funded.

Chapter 12

Creating a World-Class Research Institute

- *Ensure uninterrupted financial support.*

- *Attract the very best and most enthusiastic scientists.*

- *Provide state-of-the-art laboratory space, equipment, and technical support.*

- *Create an innovative, focused, scientific approach.*

- *Organize international symposia.*

- *Increase public understanding of science.*

To ensure that the Institute would be financially independent forever, I wanted to be sure that it would follow the principles that enabled me to build American Century. My philosophy has always been that it is essential to never spend your capital – it is the seed money. Only income should be spent. My belief is that the greatest menace to the value of capital is inflation, not the risk of investing in common stocks. The stock market goes up and down, but we must stay fully invested, no matter what.

Coincident with beginning our recruitment of independent investigators, our laboratory leaders, it was crucial that we recruit outstanding leaders of technology. Their technical expertise and knowledge of how to apply it to biology are essential for ground breaking research results.

Bill Neaves

Chapter 12

To enable the Institute to perform **endowment-based scientific research**, we set up the following rules:

Place all gifts in an endowment within the Institute.

Have the endowment professionally managed as a long-term investment.

Spend only 3.5 percent of the endowment each year for medical research.

PROTECTING THE ASSETS OF THE INSTITUTE

Following this approach, the endowment in common stock of American Century Companies should grow in value providing more money for science every year. In March 2001, the remainder of our American Century class A common stock was valued at $1.2 billion. Virginia and I decided to donate these shares to the Stowers Institute in exchange for an annual annuity which will be paid until both of us have died. We began receiving this annuity in January 2006 when our initial gift had grown to $2 billion.

But where would we like the assets of the endowment invested for the long-term? With all the experience and knowledge that I have acquired over 50 years in the mutual fund business, why not create a fantastic, unique fund? Such a fund would be open to everyone, offer all of the latest services, enjoy the outstanding investment management of American Century, have a unique investment approach and objective, and include an innovative feature that I believe would improve long-term investment performance.*

This fund would be an "Investor Fund" in which the investors are the ones who actually determine what can and cannot be done. The Stowers System would play an extremely important role in the investment management of this new fund's assets.

*See Appendix II for more detailed information about this innovative concept.

Chapter 12

HOPE SHARES: SEED MONEY FOR SCIENCE

Many people have been touched by our commitment to create a research center that can lay the groundwork for breakthroughs in health care. To give others a chance to participate in making our dream a reality, we created a new concept in giving: *Hope Shares*.

Unlike the usual annual giving drives where contributions are spent, 100 percent of the value of each gift contributed goes directly into the Stowers Institute endowment. Just like the money Virginia and I have contributed, these gifts are **seed money**, meaning only a portion of the gift will be spent every year to support the Institute.

For every gift of $1,000 or more, a Hope Shares account is established with the Stowers Institute. When you acquire Hope Shares, you will get the satisfaction of watching the value of your gifts grow and contribute to the endowment far beyond their original value because the Institute spends only 3.5 percent of its endowment annually. Therefore, each contribution will be a living gift that will continue to help humanity forever.

The gift will live beyond your lifetime and will express your love for family and friends to whom you have given the opportunity for a longer, healthier life. The Stowers Institute will take a unique approach in recognizing your gifts by reporting to you each year how much your gift has grown beyond its original amount. In addition, you will be informed in simple, understandable language about the progress of the Institute's scientific efforts.

You will be remembered forever for your gift.

Chapter 12

FIVE YEARS OF PROGRESS

Since the first research laboratories opened in November of 2000, The Stowers Institute for Medical Research has become recognized as one of the best research institutions in the world. The 2005 Annual Report indicated that the Institute's assets had grown to over $2 billion. There are now a total of 360 scientists and technologists working there daily.

By the end of 2005, we were more than halfway to our goal of filling our 600,000 square foot facility. Bill Neaves and Robb Krumlauf continue to search for excellent biomedical researchers and technological support staff to fill an additional 15 labs. At the moment, the Institute focuses on four main research areas: stem cell biology, developmental genetics, chromosome dynamics and regulation of gene expression.

Virginia and I feel very blessed to have Robb Krumlauf as our scientific director.

Robb is a terrific scientist, but he is also the best exemplar of collegiality that I've ever known in my career in science. Robb is a role model for collegiality combined with scientific excellence.

Bill Neaves

We are also truly grateful to have had Bill Neaves' guiding hand from the very beginning. After Bill asked us if he could take on the role of president and CEO of the Institute, we really felt that somebody up there was watching and helping us. We could not be more fortunate in our choice of leaders. They believe in our vision and our values and are creating an organization where it can truly be said that ***The Best Is Yet To Be***.

Chapter 12

The Stowers Institute's Annual Report of 2005 quoted Robb Krumlauf:

Basic biomedical research is a painstaking process of unraveling the mysteries of the human body, one by one. It happens in thousand of laboratories around the world and results in a collective knowledge that allows researchers to build upon one work to further the understanding of human health.

I am honored that research we have done has been valuable to other scientists. I believe that all scientists stand on the shoulders of giants, because we all depend on the creative work of our colleagues to inspire our curiosity and our desire to understand nature.

Robb Krumlauf and Bill Neaves

Chapter 12

HOPE FOR LIFE

When I saw the original miniature display of the future Stowers Institute campus, I felt something was missing: a visual symbol that would express the Institute's mission. I asked Larry Young, a well-known sculptor, to create a statue that would incorporate both the double helix and the human form to symbolize **Hope for Life***.*

The 31-foot, gleaming, stainless steel sculpture he created now graces the front lawn of the Stowers Institute. Suspended in the open space between two strands that make the double helix, one can imagine the human form. This striking statue is an ideal symbol of the Institute's mission to offer hope for a better life.

Jack Jonathan

Chapter 12

Hope For Life: focal point of the Stowers Institute campus.

BioMed Valley

———

*My wife, Virginia, and I dream of a time
when, within 25 years, this region of the country
will be recognized as one of the best places
in the world for basic biomedical research.*

This is our BioMed Valley Dream.

Chapter 13

THE BIG STORY

The Stowers Institute for Medical Research has been in the forefront since 1994. From the beginning, it was our dream that, within the next 25 years, this region of the country would be recognized as one of the best places in the world for basic biomedical research. A state line runs through the Kansas City area dividing Missouri and Kansas. We envisioned the Greater Kansas City area being unified by a biomed industry called BioMed Valley.

We hope that BioMed Valley will provide the inspiration, monetary resources and guidance needed for partner research institutions to create environments similar to the Stowers Institute. This will attract more talent to the area and increase the pace of discoveries.

ORGANIZATIONAL STRUCTURES

To coordinate the scientific efforts of the Stowers Institute for Medical Research and the universities in the area, we created a non-profit company, BioMed Valley Corporation. The purpose of this company is to encourage both the University of Missouri-Kansas City and the University of Kansas to establish a distinguished group of scientists who, along with the Stowers Institute, would become BioMed Valley Research Partners. The scientists of all the research partners would have to meet the same strict standards of the Stowers Institute's scientists.

BioMed Valley Corporation is the true heart of the research partnership. One of its roles is to rally the community and the research partners toward a common goal, while raising substantial endowments to

Chapter 13

support biomedical research at each of the participating institutions. To ensure adequate funding for the partners, BioMed Valley Corporation established an individual endowment within the corporation for each research partner and will pay each partner 3.5 percent of their endowment each year. The research organization of each of these partners is supervised by a Scientific Advisory Board.

Although the Stowers Institute is primarily a research institution, it is also a key member of the Kansas City Area Life Science Institute (KCALSI), a nonprofit organization created in 2000 to promote collaborative research between its ten stakeholder institutions and also to facilitate the transformation of that research into commercial ventures.

Kansas City Area Development Council

THE SCIENTIFIC ADVISORY BOARD

The importance of the Scientific Advisory Board (SAB) can not be overstated. This group actually sets the standards for scientific excellence and is determined to maintain them at a very high level.

Each member of the SAB will be internationally recognized as an outstanding scientist and is a member of the National Academy of Sciences. They unanimously approve the hiring and retaining of all new principal scientists, review their research each year, give suggestions and determine who will be given a new term of appointment. They demand great science and absolutely expect excellent scientific results.

Chapter 13

BioMed Valley Discoveries Inc.

We are extremely optimistic that the Stowers Institute and the other Research Partners will make a significant contribution to science over time. New discoveries in science often have unexpected spin-offs that can lead to commercially useful products.

However, an extremely important point had been overlooked: we had not thought of who was going to patent, develop and market our scientific discoveries. That left the Institute with the responsibility of providing that service, which takes valuable time and money away from scientific research at the Stowers Institute.

To solve this challenge, we had to create a new company. In anticipation, we formed BioMed Valley Discoveries, Inc. as a for-profit company whose mission is to find the best commercial home for new discoveries. It will have the exclusive right to seek, patent, develop, license and market all the discoveries arising from the laboratories of its research partners. These exclusive rights will be perpetual. This agreement will significantly increase the value of the stock of BioMed Valley Discoveries, Inc.

As it develops, BioMed Valley Discoveries, Inc. will benefit the Research Partners. However, BioMed Valley Discoveries will go as far from Kansas City as necessary to find discoveries worthy of commercialization.

In 2004, the Nature Publishing Group in London added
Robb Krumlauf and Olivier Pourquie, two Stowers researchers,
to a list of scientists who have made the 24 most important
discoveries in developmental biology in the past century.

Kansas City Area Development Council

Chapter 13

WHY BIOMED VALLEY DISCOVERIES, INC.?

In an attempt to attract the very best scientists, the Institute offered to compensate each with 50 percent of the profits from any of their discoveries. With the help of this commercial wing of BioMed Valley Corporation, the scientists of the Stowers Institute and the other Research Partners are reassured that there is an excellent company especially created to patent, develop and market any discoveries that may arise from their research. This will enable the scientists to focus on their basic biomedical research while still being rewarded with some of the profits derived from their discoveries. The remaining 50 percent of the profits will be kept by BioMed Valley Discoveries to increase its value.

AN INNOVATIVE WAY TO PRIVATELY FUND SCIENTIFIC RESEARCH FOREVER

The future growth of biomedical research can be assured when the endowment is not dependent on government grants, but on the initiative of people who believe in supporting the scientific effort through gifts to the Research Institute.

In Appendix I, you can read the details of a new way to privately fund scientific research by leveraging these gifts and the future value of scientific discoveries to create an endowment that will continue to fund research forever.

Chapter 13

CONCLUSION

I am convinced that BioMed Valley can become recognized as the best place in the world for basic biomedical research. This can be accomplished if enough of us in the Kansas City community are determined to make this dream become a reality. The success of the Stowers Institute for Medical Research is proof that world-class scientists will come to Kansas City. They are excited to be able to do their research in a collegial, well-funded, well-equipped environment. The knowledge that their discoveries will be converted into useful products to help people is an added incentive.

The question remains, will the Kansas City community rally behind this opportunity? Much more needs to be done if this region of the country is to be recognized as one of the best places in the world for basic biomedical research. We must unite the research institutions and ensure that all maintain the highest standards of scientific excellence.

We must find a way of converting the extraordinary value of future scientific discoveries into additional assets that will support even more basic biomedical research. A biotech industry would enable critical breakthroughs to be patented and marketed so that scientific discoveries could truly help all mankind to live a healthier life.

What is most exciting about BioMed Valley is the transformational character that it represents for the region. We use the word "region" because geographically this area is a river valley that includes two states: Missouri and Kansas. So to be inclusive, Jim named the region BioMed Valley.

Jim is a patient man and thinks about the long-term implications of what he is doing. What very few people grasp is the literally century-long view that Jim and Virginia have for transforming this region.

They see the future of the Institute and BioMed Valley beyond their lifetime and beyond our lifetimes.

Dick Brown

What I have Learned

After I reflected on what I have learned over time, I became firmly convinced that anyone, and I do mean anyone, can become what they are absolutely determined to be. I became successful by trying to help people improve their financial position.

I built American Century using the following principles. You, too, can succeed if you:

- Admit to yourself, and convince others, that you do not know all the answers.
- Surround yourself with the very best people, people who know more than you do.
- Offer only the very best product or service that people want and need – not the second best.
- Maintain your advantage by offering only unique services and products that are difficult or almost impossible for others to duplicate.

You will discover that the best solutions to problems are reached through the extraordinary power of teamwork. It is extremely important to note that decisions arrived at as a result of team discussions are far more effective than those made by any one individual.

Mountains can be moved if team members share the same values and focus on the same goal. Remember, a chain is only as strong as its weakest link.

Virginia and I wanted to give back something more valuable than money to the millions of people who made our success possible. We wanted people to be able to look forward to enjoying a healthy life. That is why we created the Stowers Institute for Medical Research using the same principles that helped American Century become successful.

The Institute opened its doors on the first of the year 2000, and it is already recognized as one of the best institutions in the world for basic biological research.

Please share with us our firm belief that, ***The Best is Yet to Be.***

Appendices

Appendix I

THE ORGANIZATIONAL CHART
BIOMED VALLEY CORPORATION AND
BIOMED VALLEY DISCOVERIES, INC.

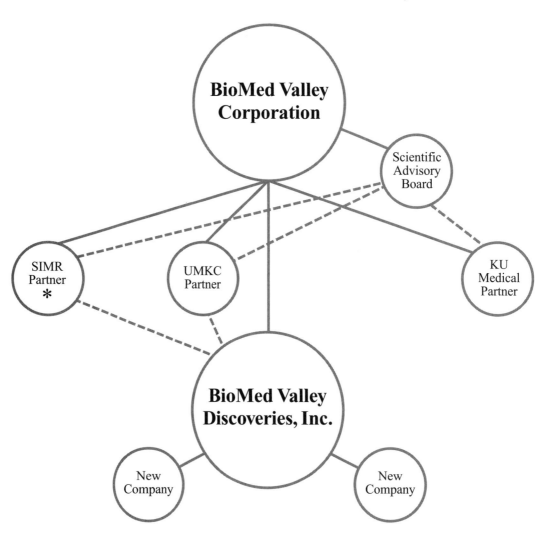

✱ (SIMR) Stowers Institute for Medical Research.

Appendix I

BioMed Valley: Raising Capital for Scientific Research

The Stowers Institute for Medical Research gave $60,000,000 to BioMed Valley Corporation, which used $10,000,000 for its working capital. A new for-profit company, BioMed Valley Discoveries, Inc., was created to patent, develop and market scientific discoveries of all the Research Partners. BioMed Valley Corporation bought all its 50,000,000 shares with the remaining $50,000,000 (received 6,000 shares Class B stock with 10,000 votes per share and 49,994,000 shares Class A with one vote per share).

This capital structure permits BioMed Valley Corporation to generate additional funding for basic cell and molecular biology research in BioMed Valley through the sale of its Class A stock over time.

In the future, BioMed Valley Corporation plans to sell all of its Class A stock in BioMed Valley Discoveries Inc., retain all of the Class B shares and pay all the proceeds from that sale to the various BioMed Valley Research Partners' endowments within BioMed Valley Corporation.

The Importance of the Endowments

The endowments will be professionally managed by American Century Investments and invested for long-term appreciation. Based upon historical data, the endowments should at least double every ten years, ensuring a growth over time at a rate substantially in excess of 3.5 percent.

The size and value of the combined endowments of the BioMed Valley Research Partners, along with the endowment of Stowers Institute for Medical Research, are extremely important.

The value of the initial endowments was $1,371,554,564; 3.5 percent of which was earmarked for scientific research ($48,004,758).

Appendix I

In 25 years, the endowment is expected to appreciate to $10,850,560,839; 3.5 percent of that amount would be spent for scientific research, totaling $379,769,629 that year.

Research Partners must spend 3.5 percent of the value of their individual endowments each year on scientific research. The value of the combined endowments determines the amount of money that will be available for scientific research each year. As the size of the endowments increase in value, the amount of money spent on scientific research also increases. Great things are bound to happen as the endowment grows and more exceptional scientists are attracted to work in the labs. These scientists, working as a team, can increase the rate of their successful discoveries.

BioMed Valley Discoveries, Inc., will have an exclusive, perpetual, worldwide license to all of the discoveries ever made by the research partners. The scientists will be compensated with 50 percent of the profits from their discoveries. BioMed Valley Discoveries, Inc. will retain the remaining 50 percent of the profits from the patenting and marketing of discoveries which will increase the value of BioMed Valley Discoveries, Inc. stock.

How Much is the Stock of BioMed Valley Discoveries, Inc. Worth?

It is important to learn why BioMed Valley Discoveries, Inc. is so valuable to the success of the entire effort. Let us consider these questions:

- What percentage of the total amount actually spent on all science will likely produce discoveries?

- How much money will actually be spent on science over time?

On the first point, we found a study of 50 colleges. With millions of dollars spent on science at various universities, we learned that, on average, only 5.9 percent of all that money is spent on science-produced discoveries.

Appendix I

On the second point, in order to select a percentage rate of return to be used in our calculation, we looked at the average rate-of-return received on American Century Growth shares from June 1971 to the end of 2005. That percentage was 15 percent rate of return over 33.5 years. Arbitrarily, we lowered that 15 percent down to 12.5 percent. We assumed that the endowments would all grow at a rate of 12.5 percent rate each year over time. Each year, 3.5 percent of the value of the endowments would be spent on scientific research.

The amount that was spent on science was calculated for 100 years. We then assumed that only 5.9 percent of the entire amount produced scientific discoveries. One-half of that amount had previously been paid directly to the scientists who made the discoveries. The remaining amount, which represented BioMed Valley Discoveries, Inc.'s portion, was then discounted to the present time using a 5 percent rate. That figure amounted to $661,462,333.

The initial capital of BioMed Valley Discoveries, Inc. was $50,000,000. The value of that company will increase from $50,000,000 to $710,561,300. The value of each share of that company thus will increase from $1.00 to $14.23, a 14.23 to one leverage.

These assumptions will immediately convert the extraordinary value of future scientific discoveries into additional assets for basic cell and molecular biology research.

Instead of trying to sell all of the Class A stock of BioMed Valley Discoveries, Inc. **now** and causing BioMed Valley Corporation, which owns the shares, to pay the proceeds received from the sale of $710,000,000 to the various endowments of the BioMed Valley Research Partners for more research today, why not try something truly fantastic? Why not use the shares of BioMed Valley Discoveries, Inc. as an enticement to encourage people to give money to one of the endowments of BioMed Valley Corporation?

Appendix I

If a person gives at least $100,000 to one of the endowments, why not allow that person to also participate directly in the success of BioMed Valley Discoveries, Inc. by paying an additional ten percent of the gift (in this case $10,000) to buy the Class A shares of that company from the owner of those shares, BioMed Valley Corporation, at its present value? That would be a ten to one leverage. **All of the proceeds from both of these transactions would be given to the endowments within BioMed Valley Corporation.**

When the time comes that all the Class A stock are sold, over $7 billion (not $7 million) will have been added to the endowments. This is truly a unique way of building endowments for scientific research.

To demonstrate how this opportunity works, my wife, Virginia, contributed $5,000,000 to BioMed Valley Corporation. $2 million was to be allocated to each university endowment account of the University of Missouri - Kansas City and the University of Kansas. An additional $1,000,000 was to be given to the Stowers Institute endowment account. All are within the BioMed Valley Corporation. She took a tax deduction on her $5,000,000 gift.

Virginia also took advantage of the option to invest ten percent of the $5,000,000 gift she had given to the BioMed Valley Research Partners endowments. That meant that she could buy $500,000 in the Class A shares of BioMed Valley Discoveries, Inc. from BioMed Valley Corporation at the value at that time, $14.23 a share. The shares will be registered in the name of Stowers Institute for Medical Research and delivered to the Institute. Virginia made a gift of those shares to the Institute because the law did not permit her to own the stock in her own name. The purchase price of $500,000 was added to the Stowers Institute's Research Partners' endowment account within BioMed Valley Corporation.

Appendix I

Leveraging the Value of Future Scientific Discoveries with BioMed Valley Registered Fundraisers.

The BioMed Valley concept is an absolutely fantastic idea. It gives a group of fundraisers the opportunity to make people aware of how they can use a unique way of funding science that will improve the quality of everyone's lives and, at the same time, be remembered forever for doing it. It is an innovative way of privately funding scientific research forever.

The Registered Fundraiser promotes the funding of science for the Investigators who are members of the two university research partners in BioMed Valley.

Compensation of BioMed Valley Registered Fundraisers.

- On a sliding scale, receives from ten percent on gifts of $1,000 to $10,000, to two percent on $2,000,000 and larger gifts.

- Receives 20 percent of the compensation for any person who is encouraged to become a Registered Fundraiser and is approved by BioMed Valley Corporation.

This is truly a salesman's dream. Everyone wins. This will probably be the way science is funded in the future.

Appendix II

PROTECTING THE ASSETS
OF THE INSTITUTE

The Stowers System Advantage

The Stowers System plays an extremely important role in the investment management of the Institute's assets. It actually determines which stocks **can be bought** and which stocks **can continue to be owned**.

The portfolio managers must invest only in those companies whose earnings and revenues **are growing** at an accelerated rate. They are not to invest in those **anticipated** to grow at an accelerated rate.

When the earnings and revenues of those companies **stop** growing at an accelerated rate, the portfolio managers are expected to sell all, not part, of those stocks because those stocks have become "hot potatoes." In short, I want **all** of the stocks in the portfolio to have accelerating earnings and revenues.

I would like to have the Institute's assets managed through a new mutual fund that uses this strategy and some additional, innovative concepts that are discussed below. However, to date, we have not been successful in convincing the Securities Exchange Commission to allow us to incorporate these additional concepts into a publicly offered mutual fund.

A New Fund Concept – Dealing with an unintentional flaw

Over time, investors have treated mutual funds exactly as if they were individual stocks which could be bought and sold on the same day.

However, there is one major, unintentional flaw in the logic of the mutual fund concept. When investors buy funds, they automatically share in

Appendix II

the costs required to invest their money in portfolio securities because they are in the fund at that time. But when investors want to liquidate their investment, those investors do not share in the costs to convert portfolio securities into cash because they are no longer in the fund at that time.

More importantly, these investors do not share in the significant market risks when portfolio securities are converted into cash, especially during a down market. In other words, the liquidating investor forces the remaining investors in the fund to pay all the brokerage costs and take any loss from market risks. These costs, especially the loss in value due to market risk, absolutely reduce the long-term funds' investment performance for the remaining investors.

An Extreme Example

Assume an investor has a $50 million investment in individual securities **in the stock market** at a time when the market begins to fall drastically, 1,000 points a day. The investor panics and wants to instantly sell his entire $50 million investment portfolio. He calls his broker to request the entire investment be sold. The broker attempts to sell the securities. The market value of the stocks continues to fall rapidly each day. In time, the broker sells the stocks at prices much lower than the prices at the time the sell order was first placed. Let us assume the investor receives only $40 million net. The investor lost $10 million, including the entire brokerage fee. This represents the normal way an individual stock investor pays for his investment costs.

Now, let us assume this same investor had his $50 million assets in a mutual fund. The investor could panic and ask that all of his investment be liquidated. He could require the fund to pay him the value the fund was worth at the close of market on the day he requested the sale. Assume that

Appendix II

value was $50 million. Realize that the fund would not be able to even start selling portfolio securities for this liquidation until the market opened the following day.

The market had fallen 1,000 points the previous day. Let us assume it fell the same amount the second day. The fund would then be forced to sell many more of its securities at prices much lower than the previous day's close. The mutual fund owed the investor $50 million, so it had to sell even more stocks at lower prices in order to accumulate $50 million. Since the investor *was no longer in the fund*, the remaining shareholders in the fund had to pay and absorb all of the costs. The remaining shareholders in the fund also had to absorb all of the brokerage costs to sell securities. They also had their long-term investment record damaged. This is the way mutual funds presently operate. This is the normal scenario for selling mutual funds.

In this case, this investor received $50 million from the fund while the remaining fund shareholders had to absorb the $10 million loss including all the brokerage costs. **Is this fair?**

Making Fund Redemption Fair for All

I am determined to try to correct this flaw in the logic of the "mutual fund concept." I believe the only way to practically remove this one major flaw is **to force all fund investors who wish to sell shares to remain shareholders inside the fund long enough to automatically share in the costs of converting portfolio securities into cash and to pay brokerage fees.**

Here is my proposal of how to make fund redemptions fair to all:

- Inform potential investors exactly what the fund liquidation policies are that must be followed by fund shareholders.

Appendix II

- Have everyone who is interested in buying the fund shares sign a statement ahead of time that they are willing to give the fund **seven business days'** notice for any liquidation or exchange to another fund, regardless of market conditions.*

- If an investor refuses to sign this statement, that investor would not be given the opportunity to invest.

This would be best for everyone. Investors would share in their own costs to liquidate their investment, and they could not force the fund to exacerbate stock market reactions.

If an investor complains in the future about having to wait the seven business days, the fund can present him with a copy of his initial signed statement. That should end the controversy.

---

* At this time, the Securities and Exchange Commission will not allow us to offer a mutual fund to the public if it includes this kind of notice requirement.

Appendix III

Enjoying the Very Best

The Yellow Motor Home

In 1973, I read that GMC had built a new motor home that didn't look like a box – it was streamlined. A video at the dealer showed the motor home driving over a train track. The body remained absolutely level while the front wheels and the back tandem wheels bounced up and down. The motor home had torsion bar front-end suspension and air ride in the rear. It was very impressive. The motor home came in two sizes, 18 feet and 26 feet in length.

I was extremely impressed and determined quickly that I just had to have one of the larger ones. But how could I convince Virginia that we really needed to buy one? I immediately thought that our company could use one to demonstrate our new computer system to various portfolio managers around the country. As an added benefit, we could easily use it to take the family on trips to Florida and California.

I ordered a yellow motor home to be ready for the first quarter of 1974 with the understanding that we would pick it up directly at the factory. I did not want anyone driving my motor home at 80 miles an hour from the factory, driving over curbs like I had seen them do at the dealership. Since this was not standard practice, I had to insist that if they wanted my order, I had to pick it up directly at the factory. They finally agreed.

The selling price of the motor home was around $24,000. I was able to negotiate a purchase price of under $13,500 because, at that time, the price of gasoline was climbing up rapidly. The dealer was afraid that he might not sell very many motor homes, so he gave me a great deal for a fantastic motor home.

Appendix III

I went home to share with my wife, Virginia, what I had done. She was shocked at the news. She made it clear to me that she would never sleep in that motor home. I answered by saying, "Virginia, you just don't understand. I plan to drive the motor home up to a hotel, let you and the kids out, and I will park it. It is for ease of transportation only." My wife, who was raised in Wyoming, was convinced that she had experienced all the camping she ever wanted.

In the spring of 1974, Virginia, an officer of our company and I flew to Michigan to pick up the motor home. We drove to the factory. While we were waiting, we watched as many of the motor homes were being moved around. Virginia noticed that most of the drivers were women. That impressed her.

After waiting for awhile, they informed us that the motor home that had been built for us had mistakenly been sent to a dealer in Flint, Michigan. They asked if we would be willing to deliver one to that dealer and exchange it for the one that had been built for us. We agreed and drove a new motor home to Flint to exchange for the one built for us.

Our 26-foot, streamlined motor home was painted yellow. It had torsion bar suspension in the front end and air ride tandem suspension in the rear. It had an extremely soft ride and drove like a dream. You could place a glass of water on the tray beside the driver and it would remain there and not spill. It was fantastic and lots of fun to drive.

Back in Kansas City, we placed a computer terminal and a modem in it so an officer of the company could drive it around to different locations in the center part of the country, demonstrating our computer service to various portfolio managers. We hooked the computer up by telephone line to our company computer in Kansas City.

Appendix III

But our timing was quite bad. The stock market had a big reaction that lasted a long time.

Although we demonstrated the system to many people, no one showed any interest at that time.

After having watched several women driving the motor home at the factory, my wife was eager to learn how to drive it. If those women could drive it, so could she. I wanted to make sure she knew how to park it. We went to a large school parking lot and I showed her how to parallel park the motor home. She tried over and over and learned it well.

We took many trips in it with the family, several to Florida. We would pull up to a fancy hotel where we had reservations, unload the motor home, park it and spend the night in the hotel.

On one of these trips, we were driving through Tennessee. I was sleeping on the bed in the rear, while Virginia was driving. My son came back and woke me up, saying his mother was driving 80 miles an hour. I got up and went up front. Virginia said she was determined that the truck behind us was not going to pass. She was a good – and determined – driver.

On another trip to Florida, we spent several nights in Fort Lauderdale before we drove down to sight-see in Key West. It was a beautiful but long trip, going from island to island. On the return trip, we thought that we could find a nice motel to stay in. We were sorry to learn that all of the motels were full. We kept driving north, but they were all full. It was about midnight. What could we do?

We decided to drive across the state of Florida on Alligator Alley and look for a motel on the west coast of Florida. Driving across the state at that time of night was difficult because it was extremely dark. After we arrived at the coast, we had to decide whether to turn left or right. We decided to turn

Appendix III

left. It was past midnight by that time. We saw a sign saying KOA Camp Grounds. Virginia suggested we turn in to see if they had a vacancy. We drove up to the front door and parked. All the lights were out. Virginia decided we'd stay parked there and remain in the motor home all night.

We did. It was Virginia's idea. She had previously committed herself to never sleep in that motor home. Well, she did. It was the first time for her. It really wasn't that bad. The next morning we woke up hearing people walking around, but at least we had gotten some sleep.

Every summer while our family was young, we all drove in the motor home to San Diego, California to visit Virginia's mother. These trips were inexpensive vacations. Once out in California, we stayed with her mother. The kids went to the ocean every day, wore themselves out playing in the water, came home, ate dinner and then crashed in bed. Everyone had a great time. It took three days to get to California and three days to return home.

At our home in Kansas City, we parked the motor home in the back of our house on the side of the driveway. It was electrically connected to our home for power and it could be connected through the home telephone line to the company office. When the company was extremely busy, my wife would go to the motor home and help enter customer transactions directly into the company computer.

Once, the weather got bad. We had an ice storm and electrical lines were knocked down causing our home to lose electric power. We rewired the electrical connection to our motor home so that it could supply electricity to our house. The motor home had a 6,000 watt generator. It provided enough electricity for one room to have the lights on and provide for the TV. This worked out well because the electricity did not come back on for about two weeks.

Appendix III

Our last trip to California in the motor home was in 1986. There were only the two of us. After our three-day trip home, I turned into our driveway and parked our big yellow vehicle. I asked Virginia what was the first thing she wanted me to do. She said that she would like me to put a "For Sale" sign on the motor home. When I asked why, she stated, "I would rather enjoy spending six days on the beach than six days riding in this motor home." I thought a moment about her answer. I couldn't disagree with her.

Sierra Aviation

I thought to myself, what is going to be our future means of transportation to California? It must be fast so my wife could spend more time on the beach. What about an airplane? That wasn't such a bad idea. I had been a fighter pilot in the Air Force, but I hadn't flown for some time.

The next day I went to the office and announced that I would ask the executive committee to buy a jet airplane. Several days later, at the executive meeting they were really prepared for me. They had looked up all of the airline travel expenses for the previous year, which amounted to $15,000. While the original motive was my family's convenience and my love of flying, I felt that the time wasted by the executives traveling via commercial airlines was also valuable. They asked me how I could justify having the company buy a plane.

I answered, "If the company buys a jet airplane, I will agree to pay all the expenses of the plane for two years." They couldn't resist. They bought a plane. However, I paid the expenses for three years, not two. I knew if they once experienced all the convenience of using the plane in business, they would always justify having one.

Appendix III

We named the company that owned the plane Sierra Aviation.

For Sierra Aviation to provide a safe method of transportation, we needed:

- A plane with a solid, well built airframe.

- The best qualified pilots.

- Outstanding maintenance.

In September 1986, the company acquired a ten-year old Falcon 20 made by the French company, Dassault. It could hold six passengers. At the same time, we hired the flight crew that had previously flown the plane.

I had been trained as a fighter pilot in the Air Corps in World War II and had accumulated over 1,200 hours flying time. However, I had not flown jets for about 23 years. To get recurrent in flying jets, I attended a Flight Safety course for the Falcon in New Jersey along with my son, Jim, who had acquired some flying experience while in college. While our Sierra flight crew would normally pilot the plane, Jim and I also wanted to be able to fly the plane whenever we took a trip.

The Falcon 20 was extremely well-built and handled like a fighter. It introduced the members of our company to the advantages of corporate aviation. Its range of flight was around 1,000 miles. Since many of our trips where greater than that, we sometimes had to dip down to refuel which increased the flight time to our destination.

We kept the Falcon 20 for a little more than two years. Originally we paid $1,200,000 for the plane, added around $350,000 for improvements and sold it for the same amount we paid for it.

Appendix III

To replace it, we searched for an outstanding plane that could fly internationally and carry more passengers. We located an extremely clean, low-flight time Lockheed Jet Star II, which had been used solely by the president of a company. We bought it sight unseen in May of 1988. It was very well built, with two large external fuel tanks under the wings and four jet engines. We spent about a half million dollars to improve the plane's quality so that it would be recognized as one of the best Jet Star II's flying.

The Jet Star served us well, however, the engines were old technology and used a lot of fuel. The cabin space was also crowded and the instruments in the cockpit were mechanical, not electronic.

Originally we paid $2,500,000 for the plane, added about $500,000 for improvements and sold the plane after two years for $4,000,000 in November of 1990 for top dollar.

Walt Day, our chief pilot, searched the world for a jet equipped with the latest jet engines so that we could save fuel. We also wanted a wide-body plane to provide a more comfortable space for the passengers. Walt was anxious to find the best wide-body Canadair Challenger 600 he could find. Finally, one that was in top condition was located in England.

We had the plane flown to Duncan Aviation in Lincoln, Nebraska after it was inspected in Dallas, Texas. We made major modifications. The mechanical part of the cockpit was replaced with an all glass, electronic cockpit. We also installed new navigational equipment, remodeled the cabin and had the plane repainted.

While this was happening, Walt was diagnosed with lymphoma and entered the hospital for chemotherapy. After his treatment was finished, he returned home to recuperate. Several days later, he told his doctor that he

Appendix III

wanted to travel up to Lincoln to see how the plane was progressing. The doctor did not think that was a good idea but said he could go if he was careful.

After he arrived in Lincoln and looked at the progress of the plane, Walt called me on the phone to share his enthusiasm. About 15 minutes after he talked to me, I received another phone call from his wife. She informed me that he had just died while taking a shower. What a shock! He had an embolus thrown as a result of his chemotherapy.

I was faced with the challenge of finding a new chief pilot. First, I had to determine exactly what attributes I wanted in a chief pilot. Among other things, I wrote a pilot must:

- Have over 2,000 total flying hours
  - For experience.
- Have been a fighter pilot
  - For knowledge of how to instantly recover from unusual flight positions.
- Have a master's degree from college
  - For education.
- Be a leader and team player.

Where could I find a person with these qualifications?

I asked Bruce Jefferies, an employee of American Century who had previously been an officer in the Air Force, if he could find someone who would fit my requirements.

To my surprise, the next morning he presented me with an ideal candidate, Colonel John Small, who was retiring from the Air Force. John had been test flying the B-2 at Edwards Air Force Base and had more flying time testing the B-2 than any other pilot at that time.

Appendix III

John became the chief pilot of our Canadair Challenger 600. He was really excited about the plane's quality. When he talked to his former Air Force pilots at Edwards, they were enticed to ask Sierra Aviation to trade flying time with them. So we arranged for their pilots to fly the Challenger, and in return, our pilots would get some fighter time. They wanted the Air Force pilots to experience a late model commercial jet. We were proud to show off and trade flying time.

I had the privilege of flying many hours with John. He was a fantastic pilot. We became close friends.

One day, after about three years flying together, I suggested to John as we sat in the cockpit that I thought that he would make an excellent portfolio money manager. His comment was, "I am a pilot."

"That is right," I replied, "but you won't always be."

I asked John if he would like to be tested by Dr. Stan Kushner, our company psychologist, who had evaluated many of our executives. This evaluation might help John determine his interest in managing money. John agreed to be tested.

After the test, Dr. Kushner rushed into my office exclaiming "John sets the curve for the entire company." He said that he asked John to recite a long list of numbers. John recited the numbers accurately, however in the reverse order. Stan was surprised and impressed.

Even though John had a master's degree in laser optics, our company required that he also have a MBA degree. He continued to fly for Sierra, while earning his MBA. Once he graduated, American Century welcomed him as a fund manager.

Appendix III

After Virginia and I created the Stowers Institute for Medical Research in 1994, I was practicing instrument flying, my love. Suddenly I found myself thinking about what we should be doing at the Institute. This shocked me. I was supposed to be concentrating on instrument flying. It was wrong and dangerous to think about anything else while flying. At that moment, I absolutely convinced myself that I had to get out of the cockpit and stay out. I haven't flown since, but my love for flying still remains.

Sierra Aviation encouraged another former B-2 pilot to join the company. John Belanger became our chief pilot and remains so today.

Bombardier, the company that built the Canadair Challenger 600, decided to build the "Global Express," a new, state-of-the-art, larger airplane. It was designed to fly from New York to Tokyo nonstop. I wanted the company to have one.

At this time, American Century Companies was in the process of paying a large dividend to its shareholders. I made an agreement with the company that I would allocate $40,000,000 of my dividend to the company if they would buy

Mr. Stowers,

You know that you have made an impact on many peoples' lives and I can certainly vouch for that fact!

Who would have thought that a "plain old" Air Force retiree could get one of the best aviation jobs in the world at one of the best companies, and then end up managing money. WOW!

I just want to say Congratulations on your 80th year and here's to many, many more!

Plus, thank-you so much for this wonderful opportunity at a second career! Here's to those hours together, both in the cockpit and in the office.

Whenever I see a bird, I'll always remember our sage advice to "stay humble ... those are the creatures that really know how to fly!"

Thanks for everything!

John Small

Appendix III

one of those airplanes. Furthermore, if the company flew that plane for eight years, they could do whatever they wanted with it afterwords. However, if they did not keep the plane for at least eight years, they would have to make a gift of the plane to the Stowers Institute.

In the spring of 1998, Sierra Aviation bought the Global Express. It was delivered on August 16, 2001, over three years after we had signed the papers and made the first payment.

In February 2001 we had an opportunity to sell the Challenger. Originally we paid $4,455,929 for the plane, added around $1,600,000 for improvements and sold it for $9,000,000, which was top dollar because it was one of the best around. We had flown the plane for about 11 years.

Sierra Aviation now has four pilots, a flight attendant/flight scheduler and two aircraft maintenance technicians. Two of the pilots have been B-2 pilots and one was a navy carrier fighter pilot. We have had some exciting landings!

Our Smaller Planes

Sierra Aviation bought a small jet, a Cessna Citation Bravo, in April 2000. At that time, we had no idea as to when the Global Express would be delivered. We needed a plane that could be flown on trips.

Sierra Aviation bought a Cessna Citation CJ3 on September 16, 2005 to replace the Bravo. The plane had improved electronics and better performance.

On September 30, 2005, Sierra sold the Cessna Citation Bravo. Originally we paid $5,272,925 for the plane – about 5 years later, we sold it for $4,000,000.

Appendix III

By August 2006, we will have flown the Global Express five years. Originally we paid $35,216,091 for the plane. Presently we are having "Heads Up Display" and "Enhanced Vision" installed for $1,300,000. These features were not available at the time this plane was built. If we were to sell this plane today, we could command the very top dollar, around $40,000,000.

Sierra Aviation's experience has proven my strongly held belief about investing only in the best and then maintaining its quality. This principle not only applies to airplanes but to all the capital investments. I have encouraged executives to "Buy the very best, maintain it and update it so that it increases in value over time, and then truly enjoy the use of it while it is owned."

While we continue to own this beautiful, impressive plane, we are able to truly enjoy what it provides. With our experienced pilots, we can safely travel a long way, fast, because of the plane's design, construction and sophisticated electronics. Time is saved while we travel and we can continue to enjoy the comfort, warmth and security of the cabin.

Appendix IV

AWARDS HISTORY FOR JIM AND VIRGINIA

2005   Entrepreneur of The Year National Award (JES), Ernst and Young

2005   Entrepreneur of The Year Hall of Fame Inductee (JES), Ernst and Young

2005   Entrepreneur of The Year Central Midwest Finalist (JES), Ernst and Young

2005   Honorary Doctorate of Science (JES), Washington University

2005   Kansas Citians of The Year (JES and VGS), Kansas City Chamber of Commerce

2004   Centurions Leadership Award (JES and VGS), Kansas City Chamber Centurions

2004   Honorary Doctor of Science (JES), Washington University

2004   Hope Award (JES and VGS), National Multiple Sclerosis Society

2004   Outstanding Kansas Citians (JES and VGS), Native Sons of Greater Kansas City

2004   World Citizen of the Year (JES), Kansas City Mayors United Nations Day

2003   Greater Kansas City Business Hall of Fame (JES), Junior Achievement

2003   Lance C. Wittmeyer Award (JES and VGS), Touched by Cancer Foundation

2002   175th Anniversary Honor Roll (JES and VGS), Jackson County, Missouri

2002   Annual Citation of Midwest Research Institute's Board of Directors (JES), Midwest Research Institute

2002   Excellence in Community Service (JES and VGS), Daughters of the American Revolution

2002   Outstanding Alumnus (VGS), Research Nursing Alumni Association

2002   Rex L. Diveley Chair Community Recognition Award (JES and VGS), UMKC School of Medicine

2001   Golden Plate Award (JES), American Academy of Achievement

2001   Honorary Doctor of Medicine (JES), UMKC School of Medicine

2001   Honorary Doctor of Nursing (VGS), UMKC

Appendix IV

2000   Founder's Award (JES and VGS), UMKC School of Medicine

2000   Philanthropists of the Year (JES and VGS), Greater KC Council
        on Philanthropy

1999   Chancellor's Medal (JES and VGS), UMKC

1999   Honorary Doctor of Commercial Science (JES), St. Mary's College,
        Leavenworth, KS

1999   Honorary Doctor of Humane Letters (VGS), St. Mary's College,
        Leavenworth, KS

1999   Rizzuto Award (JES), Unico

1998   Cincinnatus Award (JES), University Club of Kansas City

1998   Distinguished Civil Service Award (JES and VGS), Baker University

1998   Human Relations Award (JES), Jewish Community Relations
        Bureau/American Jewish Committee

1995   Business Person of the Year (JES), Kansas City Rotary Club

1995   Honorary Doctorate of Business Administration (JES),
        Rockhurst University

1995   Honorary Doctorate of Humanities (VGS), Rockhurst University

1995   Honorary Doctor of Humanities (VGS), Research College of Nursing

1994   Local Hero Award (JES), Ingrams magazine

1993   Outstanding Financial Executive (JES), Kansas State University

1992   Entrepreneur of the Year (JES), Henry W. Bloch School of Business
        & Public Administration, UMKC

1949   Bachelor of Science Medicine (JES), University of Missouri-Columbia

1947   Bachelor of Arts and Sciences (JES), University of Missouri-Columbia

James E. Stowers

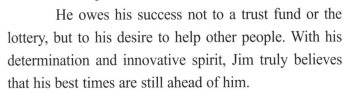

As founder and Chairman of the Board of American Century Investments, a multi-disciplined, global asset management firm, Jim is recognized as one of the country's top money managers. As such, he's had the good fortune of helping millions of people improve their financial positions.

He owes his success not to a trust fund or the lottery, but to his desire to help other people. With his determination and innovative spirit, Jim truly believes that his best times are still ahead of him.

Jim began his career when he was in his mid-twenties. It was only after more than 25 years of overcoming challenges and obstacles that his business began to prosper. Among his many innovations was his determination to help people of modest income become financially independent.

Jim wrote *Why Waste Your Money On Life Insurance* to help people understand insurance. His second book, first published in 1992, *Yes, You Can... Achieve Financial Independence*, is now in its 4th edition.

Jim and his wife, Virginia, live in Kansas City, Missouri where they have used their fortune to create one of the most important projects of their lives, the Stowers Institute for Medical Research, to give hope for a better life to millions of people.

Throughout his career, Jim's leadership has been anchored by his deep roots and values. However, he also firmly believes in surrounding himself with the very best people who work well as a team, share his vision and support his innovative approaches to making their dreams a reality.

Jack Jonathan

Jack Jonathan is an enigma. He was born in Egypt. His mother tongue was French, but he was educated in Italian. He had a classical European education and dreamed of a career in music, medicine or teaching. However, World War II intervened and changed his plans and the course of his life.

In July 1943, Jack began his career in publishing at the United States Information Agency in Cairo, Egypt. He came to the U.S. in 1952 and worked for 29 years at Hallmark Cards in product management and new product development. He was privileged to be mentored by Hallmark Cards founder Joyce Hall.

As President of Stowers Innovations, Inc., Jack continues to apply his extensive knowledge of publishing. His many recent accomplishments include creating *Yes, You Can... Raise Financially Aware Kids*, a book designed to help parents teach their children to appreciate the value of a dollar. His second book, *Yes, You Can... Find More Meaning in Your Life*, enabled him to share his enthusiasm for living a full, yet balanced life.

Although Jack is old enough to retire, he continues to follow his passion to innovate. He experiences life to its fullest and encourages others to do the same. Jack recognizes the synergy that comes from teamwork. He enjoys sharing his ideas and experiences, while helping others to do more than they think they can.

CREDITS

COVER:
Fall leaves assemblage by Kyle Larabee.

INSIDE FRONT COVER:
Photograph by James E. Stowers.

INSIDE BACK COVER:
Photograph by Stephen Helgren, PGAV Architects, with permission.

CHAPTER 3 AIRPLANE IMAGES COURTESY OF:
National Museum of the USAF: pages 69,70,71. Air Force Historical Research Agency: page 63.
Defense Visual Information Center: page 62. John Allan, Aylsham, England. Page 57.

AMERICAN CENTURY ARCHIVES:
Pages 107, 119, 122, 165, 166, 168, 172, 174, 207, page 158 (Olympic Torch) and page 159,
(Jim Stowers and Dennis von Waaden).

PAUL COKER, JR.:
Cartoons on pages 98, 100, 109, 158 and 182.

DAVE GILLESPIE:
Photographs on pages 138, 161, 190, and 203.

INGRAMS MAGAZINE:
Photograph on page 141 by Ron Berg, Ingrams Magazine, June 1992.

JACK JONATHAN ARCHIVES:
Etchings on pages 16, 18, 19, 52, 67, 83, 88 and 156.

JACK JONATHAN PHOTOGRAPHS:
Pages 52, 183, and page 158 Jim as a photographer, page 159 Jim at his organ.

KANSAS CITY BUSINESS JOURNAL:
Page 210, Bill Whitehead cartoon (March 6-12, 1998),
courtesy of the Kansas City Business Journal.

GEORGE KAUFFMAN:

Pages 176-177, Oak Tree Sequence Illustrations

MIKE MACHAT:

Page 161, painting of the Challenger flying over the American Century towers.

MONEY MAGAZINE:

page 153: photographs courtesy of Money Magazine. Cover photograph by
Greg Booth/Greg Booth & Associates Photography. Photograph of Jim jogging by Rich
Clarkson/Rich Clarkson and Associates.

STOWERS FAMILY ARCHIVES:

Spread on Jim's Dad's army career, family photos in Chapters 1, 2, 3, 4,
newspaper clippings about Stowers family stories, and
pages 91, 103, 117, 148, 159, 183, 193, 195, 198, and 200.

JAMES E. STOWERS ARCHIVES:

pages, 114, 115, 116, 123, 124.

STOWERS INSTITUTE FOR MEDICAL RESEARCH:

page 202 photograph by Ed Lallo, courtesy of the New York Times;
page 219 photograph by Dave Roche; page 220,
and 233 photographs by Don Ipock Photography;
page 231 photograph by Roy Inman.

LARRY YOUNG SCULPTURE:

photographs on pages 190 and 233

BOOK DESIGN:

Frank M. Addington